JACKIE
ROBINSON

HARVEY FROMMER

JACKIE ROBINSON

Guilford, Connecticut

An imprint of Globe Pequot

Distributed by NATIONAL BOOK NETWORK

Copyright © 1984 by Harvey Frommer
First Lyons Press paperback edition 2017

Photographs courtesy of:
UPI: pp. 15, 31, 46, 63, 70, 77, 82, 87, 92, 93, 99
The National Baseball Hall of Fame and Museum, Inc.: p. 96

British Library Cataloguing in Publication Information Available

Library of Congress Cataloging-in-Publication Data Available

ISBN 978-1-63076-157-8 (pbk.)
ISBN 978-1-63076-158-5 (e-book)

♾️™ The paper used in this publication meets the minimum requirements of American National Standard for Information Sciences—Permanence of Paper for Printed Library Materials, ANSI/NISO Z39.48-1992.

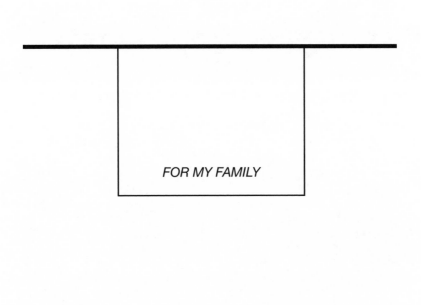

FOR MY FAMILY

CONTENTS

INTRODUCTION

When school was out, I sometimes went with my father in his taxi. One summer morning we were driving in East Flatbush down Snyder Avenue when he pointed out a dark red brick house with a high porch.

"I think Jackie Robinson lives there," he said. He parked across the street and we got out of the cab, stood on the sidewalk, and looked at it.

Suddenly the front door opened. A black man in a short-sleeved shirt stepped out. I didn't believe it. Here we were on a quiet street on a summer morning. No one else was around. This man was not wearing the baggy, ice-cream-white uniform of the Brooklyn Dodgers that contrasted against his dark skin. He was dressed in regular clothes, coming out of a regular house in a regular Brooklyn neighborhood, a guy like anyone else, going out for a newspaper and a bottle of milk.

Then incredibly, he crossed the street and came right towards me. Seeing that unmistakable pigeon-toed walk, the rock of the shoulders and hips I had seen so many times on the baseball field, I had no doubt who it was.

"Hi Jackie, I'm one of your biggest fans," I said self-consciously. "Do you think the Dodgers are gonna win the pennant this year?"

His handsome face looked sternly down at me. "We'll try our best," he said.

"Good luck," I said.

"Thanks." He put his big hand out, and I took it. We shook hands, and I felt the strength and firmness of his grip.

I was a nervy kid, but I didn't ask for an autograph or think to prolong the conversation. I just watched as he walked away down the street.

From that long ago moment and from so many times seeing Jackie Robinson magnificently ply his trade at Ebbets Field, he was always my favorite base-ball player. Driven, multi-talented, daring, he was the engine who powered the great Brooklyn Dodger team. This book, written many long years ago, was and will always be a tribute to him.

Harvey Frommer,
Lyme, N.H.
2017

THE
EARLY YEARS

1

The California dusk was still an hour away when eight-year-old Jackie Robinson, following his mother's directions, took a broom and began sweeping the sidewalk in front of their house at 121 Pepper Street in Pasadena.

"Nigger, nigger, nigger boy." The taunts of a young girl standing across the street broke the silence of the quiet afternoon. Jackie stopped his sweeping. He turned to face the white girl.

"You're nothing but a cracker," he shouted at her and began to move the broom with greater speed.

"Soda cracker's good to eat," the girl responded. "Nigger's only good to beat!"

The girl's father came out of the house. "Why don't you and your family move the heck out of here!" he shouted in an angry voice. "You don't belong in a white neighborhood."

"We do belong here," Jackie shouted back. "We have as much right to live here as you do!"

The youth's words only angered the man more. He began throwing rocks at the slim black youth. Jackie dodged a couple of the rocks, picked them up, and fired them back. One of them barely missed the man's head. The rock battle was brief. The man's wife came out and made him stop. "What kind of a hero are you?" she said to him. "Stop throwing those things. How can you take part in a rock fight with a little boy?"

Mallie Robinson, Jackie's mother, had watched the entire episode from within her modest house. She was pleased with the behavior of her youngest child. He had stood his ground. He had fought back when he had to. She was proud that despite the hardships and the prejudice, her little family was solidly together.

She thought back to a time almost eight years before, when she had cradled the infant Jackie in her arms on the crowded Jim Crow train making the long trip from Cairo, Georgia, to California. The other children—Willa Mae, Edgar, Frank, and Mack—had helped to carry the old suitcases and bags made of straw. Deserted by her husband, Jerry Robinson, Mallie realized that the new life the family was heading for would be obtained at a cost, especially on her part.

In Pasadena, Mallie had worked from dawn to dusk as a domestic. She had cut corners, saved some of the welfare money the family received, and had finally succeeded in moving herself and her children out of the crowded apartment that was their first California home to a little house.

The Robinsons survived a petition drive aimed at forcing them out of the house on Pepper Street. Mallie also rejected an offer to sell the house. And Jackie Robinson moved with his brothers and sister through the years of childhood, conscious of his mother leaving early in the morning to work for others, returning late with leftovers from the homes of the white families she worked for.

All the children were taught to look after each other. The arrangement worked well until Willa Mae began kindergarten at the Grover Cleveland School and Jackie was the only child left at home.

Mallie decided that the best plan would be for Jackie to go along to school with Willa Mae. Officials did not approve. "If I stay home and take care of Jackie," Mallie argued, "I'll have to go on relief. It'll be cheaper for Pasadena if you allow him to go along with Willa Mae and play outdoors while she's in class."

Mallie's logic convinced the authorities. So each day Willa Mae took Jackie with her. She went to classes. He played in the schoolyard's sandbox. And when the school day came to its end, Willa Mae would rejoin her youngest brother and take him home.

After a while, Jackie began to participate in the elementary school's recess sports activities. The other children would bring him sandwiches and dimes for the movies to convince him to play on their teams. "You might say," Jackie recalled in later years, "that I turned pro at an early age. I told my mother to save money by not fixing any food for me."

In the early years of Jackie's elementary school attendance, he became friends with Sidney Heard. "I began to notice," recalls Heard, who still lives in Pasadena in the old neighborhood, "that Jackie had something that the rest of us did not have. He was just an average student, but he loved sports and games of all kinds. And he would do things that the other kids could not do. We played dodge ball. One by one, kids would be eliminated when they were hit by the ball. Every time we played, he was left. And the games had to stop because nobody could hit him. That's when I and the others really began to notice him."

All the other Robinson children were excellent athletes, and all reinforced Jackie's skills. "All of us grew up playing together," recalls Mack Robinson, "and each one improved the other. Edgar, the oldest, was a fantastic roller skater on street skates and a fine bicycle rider and softball player. Frank, next to oldest, was just like a father to Jack. He was a sprinter. He was faster than I was in the hundred-yard dash, and I was a tenth of a second off the world record in those days. Willa Mae was first string on everything that girls could play in those days—basketball, track, soccer. She was also a top sprinter in her day. Jack got his start in long jumping from me. He was a combination athlete. He was great in all sports. I saw that from the time he was in junior high school."

The California weather was almost always moderate. It was an area ideal for outdoor games all year round. Pepper Street was just about a mile from the Rose Bowl Stadium construction site. Sidney Heard's father and Edgar Robinson, Jackie's brother, helped build the immense stadium. Sidney Heard recalls that he and Jackie would go to the Rose Bowl site "when it was just a half bowl." There they would chase rabbits and play hide-and-go-seek and other children's games. And Jackie would talk about the day when he would run down the field in uniform in front of thousands of fans, carrying a football—the way he now scampered with Heard at the construction site, attempting to catch rabbits.

In the street games Jackie was the star, the master competitor. "We played games we invented ourselves on the vacant lot on Pepper Street," Heard recalls. One of the games was "Over the Line." Six players competed. There were three on each side. Two left fielders and a shortstop were responsible for second and third bases. The opposing batter was required to hit the ball between second and third base. The ball had to go over an imaginary line. The batter would run, attempting to get as many bases as he could before the fielder threw the ball back over the line. There were many times when Heard and Jackie and the others played the game, using a rag ball. And all of the other kids would marvel at Jackie's speed and power and agility as he stood out in the complicated and demanding game.

"Jack," recalls Heard, "was always the leader, the one to choose sides. He'd always pick the younger kids, the kids with less ability, and he'd always in all the games figure a way to beat the older kids. He always figured things out so that we'd all get a chance to play, to compete, and to have a good time."

Washington Junior High School and Cleveland Junior High School would meet each year for the Pasadena championship. Heard, who went to Cleveland Junior High School, recalls that his school could never defeat Washington Junior High. "We were always second because of Jackie," says Heard. "He made their teams something else."

Players on opposing teams always attempted to get Jackie Robinson angry to make him lose his concentration. The technique never worked. "Jackie was interested in the games," recalls Heard, "in winning, not in anything else. The madder you made him, the better he played. He never did start a fight. He could fight real well, but he would never take advantage of anyone . . . but he always looked out to never put himself in a position where he would be hurt."

Things were especially difficult for Jackie Robinson, growing up in Pasadena in the years of the Great Depression without a father. Jackie would run errands. He would water gardens and shrubs in the evenings for white homeowners. He would shine shoes for small change. He would sell hot dogs and soda at sports events, always studying the style and the skills of the competitors. A member of what was called the Pepper Street Gang—a group of kids of all races who played sports together—he would share with his friends the proceeds from the sale of golf balls he found that were hit by golfers into remote parts of courses.

A fan of the New York Yankees—especially Babe Ruth and Lou Gehrig—Jackie would read about sports as much as he could. He gave no thought to ever making it in baseball's major leagues because they were closed to blacks. Deep inside himself, however, he was sure of his athletic ability, confident that he would one day have some type of sports career.

Jackie and the other members of the Pepper Street Gang sometimes traveled long distances to compete against other "pick-up" teams.

"Wherever we played," Heard remembers, "Jackie was always the best. Grown-ups used to always come and watch us, but they came mainly to see him. He was doing things that you just don't see young kids do. And he could make any individual who played with him play much better."

As a student at John Muir Technical High School, Jackie won letters in track, football, basketball, and baseball. He was versatile and determined. Some thought he was arrogant. Others realized that he had great pride, hated to lose, and would accept nothing from himself that was less than his best effort. Coaches would conclude their pregame talks with phrases like "And if you stop Robinson, we'll have a chance to defeat John Muir Tech."

As the catcher on Muir Tech's baseball team, Robinson was selected to perform on the Pomona All-Star team in 1937. There he found himself in the company of a couple of teammates who, like himself, would go on to have legendary major-league careers—Ted Williams and Bob Lemon.

Many people were surprised that none of the major universities offered Jackie Robinson a full scholarship to get him to be part of their sports programs. The complaint against him was that he was too aggressive, too cocky, too forceful. The real reason was that most of the doors to big-time collegiate sports in that era were closed to blacks. "It just burns me up," said his brother Frank at the time, "that a Negro can't play football at places like Notre Dame. Jack can run circles around anybody in that Notre Dame backfield. Just wait . . . he'll show them all."

COLLEGE
DAYS

2

As a trim freshman in the fall of 1937 at Pasadena Junior College, Robinson was keyed up for his first football practice. He had a lot to prove. Attempting to run around left end, he was forced to the out-of-bounds line. He tried to cut back to the middle of the field but twisted his foot in a hole. He suffered a broken ankle.

Frustrated, Jackie watched from the bench as Pasadena lost its first four games. Even though his ankle was not completely healed, Jackie rejoined his team as a quarterback and led it to six straight wins and one scoreless tie.

The following fall, his ankle completely healed, Jackie led Pasadena to eleven consecutive victories and the junior college football championship. Recording over a thousand yards from scrimmage, Jackie scored 131 of his team's 369 points, including 17 touchdowns.

There was a seventy-six-yard touchdown sprint from scrimmage in the second play against San Francisco that highlighted Pasadena's 33–0 win; there was a game against San Bernardino in which he scampered for three touchdowns and passed for three others; there was a Jackie Robinson eighty-three-yard run, a field goal, and four extra points kicked in a 31–19 triumph over Santa Ana. Against Compton, which the year before had played Pasadena to a scoreless tie, he led the assault, recording two touchdowns, passing for one more.

"Jackie was the star," recalls Duke Snider, who was in the stands that day as a Compton student and who would later be Jackie's teammate on the Brooklyn Dodgers. "He wiped us out in football, basketball, baseball. He could have been a pro in all three. I still remember that game he played against Compton when he ran back that kick. He must have reversed his field three times. I think everybody on the field took shots at him, but they just couldn't touch him."

They couldn't touch Jackie Robinson in football, and he was in a class by himself in other sports as well.

On March 14, 1938, a game was staged at Brookside Park, where Jackie as a young boy once played baseball, using a tennis ball and broomstick. Now he was part of a team selected to play against major-league baseball's Chicago White Sox in an exhibition game organized to generate money for Pasadena's baseball programs. Recording two hits and making three fine fielding plays at shortstop—one of which transformed a potential run-scoring single by American League batting champ Luke Appling into a double play—Robinson showcased his skills.

"That kid is something," observed White Sox manager Jimmy Dykes after the game. "No one in the American League can make plays like that. If he were only white, I'd sign him up right now."

Years later Robinson admitted, "I wasn't surprised at all by Dykes's comment. Growing up, I really gave no thought to becoming a baseball player. I knew back then that there was no future in it for colored players. Oh, I did love softball. I played it better and played it before anything else. I was really shooting at becoming a football, basketball, or track star. But I didn't think much of a chance existed for me in baseball."

In basketball Robinson led Pasadena to the junior college championship. He was named to the All-California team.

Perhaps the most remarkable athletic accomplishment of Jackie's Pasadena Junior College career took place on May 8, 1938. On that day he starred in two different sports events in two different cities.

Arriving about an hour before the scheduled starting time for the track events in Claremont, Jackie was granted permission by the officials to engage in three broad jumps early in the meet. The plan was for him to then leave, get into a waiting car, change into his baseball uniform, and join his team in Glendale. It would be competing for the Southern California baseball championship.

"It's really nice of you," said Jackie to one of the track officials, "to allow me to do this."

"I'm looking forward to seeing what you can do," the official smiled. "I've heard a lot about you."

"Well, I hope I don't let you down, and I hope when I finish here to join my baseball team, I've still got something left so that I don't let them down."

Lean, tautly muscled, Jackie Robinson toed the mark. He pushed off down the runway. He hit the take-off board and sprang forward broad jumping for every inch he could get.

"Twenty-three feet, six inches," announced an official, thinking to himself that that would probably be the top mark for the day.

Once again Robinson toed the mark. His body was dripping with perspiration in the early California morning. He took off down the track, hit the take-off board, and thrust his body forward, landing gracefully in the soft dirt. He felt good. He knew he had exceeded the distance of his first jump. The second broad jump was measured out at twenty-four feet, six inches.

Spectators started to applaud as Jackie moved into position for his third and final jump. Every muscle in his body was poised as he ran down the runway to the take-off board and jumped with force and power and speed. It was an even farther jump than his last one. That much Jackie knew as he fumbled with a sweater to cover his torso. He watched the official draw out the tape measure.

"Twenty-five feet," announced the official, "six-and-one-half inches."

Scampering to the waiting car and the ride to Glendale, Jackie was charged up. He had broken his brother Mack's record mark for national junior college broad jumping. "Just wait," he told his friend Jack Gordon, who drove the car, "until the family learns what I did." Years later Robinson observed: "I couldn't get over it. My big brother had always been my idol, making the Olympics and all that . . . running second to Jesse Owens in the two hundred meters at Berlin in 1936."

Arriving in Glendale in the third inning of the baseball game, Jackie took his shortstop position and helped pace Pasadena to a 5–3 triumph and the baseball championship of Southern California junior colleges. It was a fitting end to his season, a season in which he batted .417, stole twenty-five bases in twenty-four games, and was voted the Most Valuable Player award in Southern California junior college baseball.

Though crowds gathered whenever Jackie Robinson put on an athletic uniform, though California newspapers gave him much coverage and coined nicknames for him such as "Dusky Flash," "Dark Demon," and "Midnight Express," though he was called the greatest all-around athlete in California sports, race was always near the surface of all Jackie was involved in.

As the lone black starter on Pasadena Junior College's basketball team, Jackie struggled to ignore the racial curses he sometimes heard shouted from the stands. In one game, a white opponent taunted and teased him. "You're a coward, Robinson," he said. "You've got no guts. You're afraid to fight me. You'll take all the crap I give you!"

"If you want to fight," Robinson responded calmly,

"we'll do it after the game. I'm not going to fight you now and hurt my team's chances of winning."

The player slammed into Robinson, flailing away with both fists. Jackie took the blows. He did not strike back. He was aware of the racial overtones that existed. The abusive player was thrown out of the game. Pasadena Junior College won not only that game but the California junior college championship as well. Robinson was named to the all-state team.

Upon graduation from Pasadena Junior College, where he had showcased his outstanding athletic skills, Robinson received many tempting offers of scholarships from colleges all over the country. "I chose UCLA," he explained, "because I planned to get a job in Los Angeles after I finished school, and I figured I'd have a better chance if I attended a local university." His major was physical education. "My mother wanted me to become a doctor or lawyer," Robinson noted, "but I never wanted to be anything but an athlete."

And what an athlete he was! He stepped up his sports accomplishments, becoming UCLA's first four-letter man. He excelled in basketball, football, and track and field. Strange as it seems, the only sport he was under par in was baseball. He batted under .200.

Jackie Robinson at UCLA was a man for all seasons, for all kinds of sports events. A standout on the UCLA basketball team, twice he led the southern division of the Pacific Coast League in scoring. He won the PCL broad-jump championship and then added the national title to his list of honors.

Jackie Robinson wins the broad-jump championship for UCLA at the Los Angeles Coliseum, May 25, 1940.

Jackie's sister Willa Mae and his childhood friend Sidney Heard remember those days at UCLA. They especially remember Jackie's competitiveness and his modesty.

"At one of the football games," notes Willa Mae, "my youngest son, Ronnie, who was then six, started to shout: 'C'mon, Uncle Jack, c'mon, Uncle Jack.' And soon the whole stadium was calling out: 'C'mon, Uncle Jack, c'mon, Uncle Jack.' I knew I was going to be in for it. Jack didn't like that kind of publicity.

"After the game he came home and I hid. 'Willa Mae,' he called out. 'Who was the one that started that Uncle Jack?'

"I said, 'I couldn't help it. What was my Ronnie going to call you?' And Jack laughed. He had a real good laugh."

Heard remembers Jackie this way: "It's just too bad that most people did not see him at his greatest, the way he was at UCLA at age twenty, like they saw Willie Mays, who came up when he was young. If Jack had gone up there when he was twenty, there'd be records they'd still be chasing . . . Whatever little flaws an individual or a team had, Jack took advantage of them. That was always his way."

His way was also the way of a poor black youth in the wealthy world of UCLA. On the gridiron or the basketball court or the baseball field or taking center stage in a track and field event, Jackie was at home. In other situations, especially social situations, the poverty of his chldhood was still a part of his makeup. The rigid social setup at UCLA further restricted him.

In 1940, twenty-one-year-old Jackie Robinson was introduced to Rachel Isum, a pretty UCLA nursing student. "I could count on my hands the number of girls I went out with before Rachel," Jackie noted. Although she was not particularly interested in sports, and a bit mistrusting of Jackie's public image in college football, Rachel nevertheless became more and more involved with the superstar UCLA athlete.

Those who knew both of them said it was a case of opposites attracting. The two fell in love even though at the start of their relationship there was not much they had in common. "Rachel became," Jackie recalled, "the most helpful and encouraging and important person I ever met in my life. When I became bitter or discouraged, she was always there with the help I needed."

In the spring of 1941, a few credits shy of a UCLA degree, Jackie was discouraged. He dropped out of UCLA. Rachel did not approve of the decision, but she understood. The financial pressures of supporting himself and his mother bore down heavily on Jackie. Other family members had pressures of their own.

"My mother had been working to support the family practically since the day I was born," Jackie explained. "She had worked herself to the point of collapse. I just can't feel right inside knowing that she needs help and not giving it when I can."

For a time Jackie worked for the National Youth Administration. He provided guidance and support for underprivileged youngsters. Ironically, he was "underprivileged" as well. Had he been white, he would undoubtedly have received offers to play professional basketball, baseball, or football. But those sports were closed to blacks. The job paid poorly and had few opportunities to offer the young man. So in the fall of 1941, Jackie left his job with the National Youth Administration and headed for Hawaii.

Weekends in Hawaii were spent playing for the Honolulu Bears, a small, semiprofessional but integrated football team. Weekdays he worked for a construction company. At last he was making enough money to help out his mother. But the football season ended quite early in Hawaii. And rather than stay on as a construction worker, Jackie headed back to the United States, where he hoped he would find something that would begin his life's work.

On December 7, 1941, aboard the *Lurline* headed for California and a reunion with his family and Rachel, Jackie saw members of the crew painting the ship's portholes and windows black. Soon afterward there was an announcement from the captain: "The Japanese have just attacked Pearl Harbor. We are heading to California with all deliberate speed. All passengers should put their life jackets on . . . just in case."

Years later Jackie would recall that voyage back home to California. At first he objected to putting on a life jacket, but when his hands began to tremble at the thought of the *Lurline* being attacked, he knew the captain had the right idea.

By the fall of 1942, Jackie, like millions of other Americans, was involved in World War II. Sent for basic training to Fort Riley, Kansas, he was classified for limited duty because of an old football injury—bone chips in his ankle. His unwillingness to accept injustice because of his race brought him into a number of controversial situations as a member of the U.S. Army.

At about the time he celebrated his twenty-third birthday in 1943, Jackie Robinson was commissioned as a second lieutenant. This achievement, however, was not earned without a struggle.

When he first applied for officers' candidate school, Robinson was told unofficially that Fort Riley's policy excluded blacks from such training. Robinson protested. He was lucky to come into contact with heavyweight boxing champion Joe Louis, who was at Fort Riley for a brief time. The most famous black athlete of that era intervened on behalf of Robinson and others like him. He brought Truman Gibson, a black civil rights leader and adviser to the secretary of defense, to Fort Riley. Gibson's presence forced openings for Jackie and several other blacks in the officers' candidate school.

As a morale officer for a provisional truck battalion, Robinson once again encountered prejudice and reacted against it. Post exchange conditions were such that black soldiers were assigned but a few seats. They were forced to stand about even when empty seats were available if those seats were restricted to use by white soldiers. Robinson protested on behalf of his men. Post exchange seating was changed to a more equitable situation. Always one to rebel against oppressive authority and injustice, Robinson's actions in the army were a continuation of his early struggles and an indication of the battles he would wage in the years to come.

BREAKING BASEBALL'S COLOR BAR

3

While Jackie Robinson and millions of other Americans were in the military service during World War II, major-league baseball continued, but at a slower pace. Most baseball executives felt that the loss of able-bodied players to the war effort was a signal for them to wait for peace before moving forward with team-building efforts. Meanwhile they made do with a patchwork assortment of players, veterans, and those with lesser skills.

Branch Rickey, newly installed as Brooklyn Dodger general manager, disagreed. At a historic meeting in January 1943 with the owners of the team, the sixty-two-year-old Rickey obtained permission from them to hire, in his words, "more scouts, to sign up fifteen- and sixteen-year olds, so the Brooklyn club will be in possession of so large a complement of youth . . . boys of all sizes and skills, that our position for the future will be secured."

A former lawyer and a lay preacher, Branch Rickey had brought with him to the Dodgers one of the most brilliant of baseball records. He had invented the farm system, an arrangement by which major-league teams either owned or had working agreements with minor-league clubs and access to their players. In his twenty-seven years in charge of the St. Louis Cardinals, he had guided the team to six National League pennants and four world championships. "Rickey," a reporter of the time observed, "could look inside a guy's muscles and see what was going on. He could spot things in a man's play, a man's run, a man's throw, that nobody else could."

On the scene now in Brooklyn, with a five-year contract of $50,000 a year, an unlimited expense account, and bonuses based on attendance, the man they called "The Brain" schemed to build a Dodger dynasty. Rickey realized that a great but untapped source of baseball talent existed— black ballplayers. A "gentlemen's agreement" existed in major-league baseball that kept the sport segregated—and the color bar that had kept tremendous talent out of the major leagues was a barrier no one through the years had had the courage or the vision to challenge.

Branch Rickey was not like other men. He knew that he and the Dodgers and especially the player who would be selected to break baseball's color barrier would suffer a great deal at the start, but he announced to the Brooklyn Dodger owners that he was going to have his scouts search "for a Negro player or two." The owners agreed to give Rickey a free hand in this pioneer venture, too.

After many conferences with his family and close associates, Rickey came up with a carefully thought out six-stage plan aimed not only at finding a black player for the Dodgers but also ensuring that the player would have as much support as possible.

The first step of Rickey's plan was completed when he met with Dodger officials. It would have been ridiculous, Rickey realized, to search for a black athlete if the ownership of the team was not prepared to support this effort.

The second step in Rickey's plan was to find a player of exceptional talent. The Dodger general manager realized that the "one" to break baseball's color barrier would have to be much more than a highly skilled performer. Rickey placed a high priority on a player who would be able to compete every day. Pitchers, therefore, were not given that high a priority. Additionally, Rickey sought a player who would be exciting, dramatic, a box-office draw—someone who could hold his own right from the start with established white baseball stars.

The third step of Rickey's master plan was to determine that the player would have the ability and the personality to meet the challenges on and off the field. Realizing that pure baseball talent would not be sufficient, Rickey was looking for a player who had fine moral character and an ability to handle himself in crowd situations and not tense up. The Dodger general manager told those close to him that he wanted a player who would be able to speak intelligently in public and at the same time be able to take abuse and suffer silently for as long as was needed. "If it comes to that," said Rickey, "and I'm sure that it will."

The fourth step of Rickey's master plan was to create a favorable press climate for the player. A veteran at handling newspaper reporters in his long years in baseball, Rickey had witnessed firsthand the power of the press. He knew that every strength and every weakness of the man chosen to break the color line would be reported in detail in the media all over the United States. Rickey was determined that the athlete be given fair treatment. Even in the planning stages of his search for the man to break baseball's color line, Rickey insisted that everything that the player had done with his life must be beyond criticism. He told his scouts that he did not want a black pioneer whose past behavior would be a target for sensationalistic reporters.

The fifth step of Rickey's plan was to enlist the cooperation of the black community. He knew that it was in their best interests as well as his—and all those who sought to break baseball's color barrier—to treat what he called the "Noble Experiment" with dignity, with caution.

The sixth step of Rickey's plan was to gain the acceptance of the player by his Brooklyn Dodger teammates. Rickey knew that the player would have a tough enough time. And he realized that if the player were made to feel part of the team, his path would be just that much easier.

The search for a black pioneer was conducted against a backdrop of sweeping social change in the United States. All over the world on battlefields, the armies of democracy opposed the forces of tyranny in the bloody struggles of World War II.

In the United States—on the streets, in the press, in the courts, and in meeting rooms—other conflicts mirrored the global struggles. Race riots broke out in 1943 in Harlem, in Detroit, and in Beaumont, Texas. President Franklin D. Roosevelt proclaimed Order 8802 that created the Fair Employment Practices Commission, an antidiscrimination group.

In December 1943 a delegation led by singer-activist Paul Robeson met with baseball Commissioner Kenesaw Mountain Landis. The delegation argued that if blacks were good enough to die for the United States fighting in the war, they should be judged good enough to play major-league baseball.

Landis replied that the employment of blacks was a decision that was to be made by individual baseball teams "without restrictions whatsoever." The statement angered black leaders. They thought it was double-talk by the commissioner of baseball and mere words issued for their public relations value. They had been witnesses through the two decades of Landis as commissioner to his opposition to allowing the color line to be crossed. In fact, Landis had banned the wearing of major-league uniforms by players who competed against Negro teams. He did this hoping to hide the fact that major-league clubs sometimes lost to Negro teams when they competed in exhibition games.

The Landis position angered the black community, but it gave hope to Branch Rickey. A longtime foe of the baseball commissioner, the Dodger general manager had battled many times with Landis in the past when he was developing the St. Louis Cardinal farm system. Now Rickey was prepared to take Landis at his public word—that the choice as to whether or not to employ blacks on major-league clubs was an individual decision to be left up to the teams. Rickey realized, however, that whatever he did would have to be done in secret, considering the climate of the time.

Rickey knew of the incident that showed the frustration of three Negro League players and their supporters; he was also aware of the negative experience of baseball promoter Bill Veeck in another instance. Yes—secretly and cautiously, Rickey decided, had to be the way to operate.

The three black players—Roy Campanella and Sam Hughes of the Baltimore Elite Giants and Dave Barnhill of the New York Cubans—according to a wire service news story on July 27, 1943, were supposed to be given tryouts with the Pittsburgh Pirates. The promised tryouts never came to be. Veeck had a plan to purchase the Philadelphia Phillies. He then was going to stock the team with black players. Landis learned of the plan and put an end to it. "We could have run away with the pennant," recalls Veeck. "I realized later that it was a mistake to have told him."

Rickey told no one about what he was doing except his inner circle. He invented a cover story to mask his activities. He said that he planned to create a new team to be known as the Brooklyn Brown Dodgers, which would play at Ebbets Field while the Brooklyn Dodgers were on the road. The Rickey plan was criticized by owners of teams in the Negro Leagues. They felt the new team would compete with them. The plan was also attacked by those who felt this was another way a major-league team was exploiting black players and keeping the color barrier up. Critics notwithstanding, Rickey forged ahead.

Scouts and aides were sent by Rickey to find a player

with exceptional athletic ability, intelligence, desire, sensitivity, and racial consciousness. The search sent Rickey's men
to Cuba, to Mexico, to Puerto Rico. Special attention was
placed on those blacks who performed in the Negro
Leagues, the only place in the United States where organized baseball competition for blacks existed.

The Negro Leagues' season ran from May to Labor Day.
A Negro National League and a Negro American League existed, each consisting of six teams. Players performed for rela-
tively low wages and under poor conditions. They sometimes
played two games in one day in two different cities, making
the move from place to place on broken-down buses. Many
of the games were played in the stadiums of major-league
teams, vacated when the big league club was on the road. In
many instances, white major-league team owners would take
40 percent of the gross of the gate receipts of Negro League
games at their ball parks.

Nevertheless, despite the poor conditions and the
segregation, the Negro Leagues had many talented players,
and Rickey made the viewing of their games a top priority for
his scouts in their search for a black pioneer.

From a baseball point of view, Rickey's scouts looked at
players with these three questions in mind: (1) Can he run?
(2) Can he throw? (3) Can he hit with power?

One of the players who was seriously considered
because he fit all three baseball categories was Josh Gibson,
a legend in the Negro Leagues. Gibson had tremendous
home-run power. However, his age and some of his personal
habits made Rickey and his scouts rule out Gibson as the
man to break baseball's color bar.

"Piper" Davis, Birmingham Black Baron infielder, was
also given serious consideration. Exceptionally swift, a fine
fielder, Davis was passed over because it was felt by Rickey
that he lacked major-league hitting ability. Satchel Paige of
the Kansas City Monarchs was a standout pitcher, but his

age and his temperament, Rickey felt, were strikes against him despite his marvelous baseball talent. "Later on," Rickey said, "after the first ones break the color bar, Paige will be able to fit in."

Catcher Roy Campanella and pitcher Don Newcombe were two others who rated high on the list of the "one" to be the black pioneer, but it was felt that they might not be able to handle all the pressure.

One player—Jack Roosevelt Robinson—was singled out by all of Rickey's scouts as the best of all the candidates. After being discharged from the army, Robinson had signed up with the Kansas City Monarchs in the Negro Leagues in April 1945 at a salary of $400 a month. It was there that his every move was measured, evaluated, analyzed.

Hall-of-Famer George Sisler, a key member of Rickey's inner circle, was highly impressed with Robinson's running skills and what he thought was Jackie's "marvelous potential as a hitter." The only negative mark Sisler gave Robinson was in the category of throwing. "His best position," Sisler told Rickey, "would be as a first or second baseman because of his average arm, but he can make the short throw well."

Other scouts came back with highly positive reports about Robinson; Rickey journeyed to California and interviewed those who had played with and against Jackie. He obtained information about Robinson's army career, the battles he had had with authorities there, standing up for his rights. The Dodger general manager liked what he heard about the strong-willed athlete. In late August of 1945, Rickey sent his trusted aide Clyde Sukeforth to do one last bit of scouting. Robinson was playing with the Kansas City Monarch team in a game in Chicago. "If you like what you see, Clyde," Rickey said, "tell Robinson that we are interested in making him a member of the Brooklyn Brown Dodgers. And bring him to me."

On August 28, 1945, at 215 Montague Street in downtown Brooklyn, New York, Jack Roosevelt Robinson, grandson of slaves, met Wesley Branch Rickey, grandson of Ohio pioneer farmers.

Both men brought to the meeting different expectations, different life experiences.

Rickey had spent thousands of dollars and almost three years searching for the "one" to break baseball's color barrier. Misunderstood by blacks who criticized him for his plan to create the Brooklyn Brown Dodgers—a team they saw as just another segregated experience—and criticized by his own family and friends for his plan to break baseball's color line, which they knew would cause him frustration and hardship, Rickey pursued his dream. The face-to-face meeting with Robinson was the climax of Rickey's three-year search. It was arranged for him to find out firsthand if Jackie had the strength of character needed for what loomed ahead.

Robinson, a 26-year-old black man searching for a place in a white world, entered Rickey's office. His days as a superathlete at UCLA were history. His time in the service had been filled with controversy because he would not knuckle under to pressure and prejudice. He was completing his season with the Kansas City Monarchs, but he was disgusted with the low wages and the living conditions. And he had promised himself that he would be quitting the Negro Leagues after the season ended. Unsettled, defensive, Robinson was not too optimistic that sports would be a way for him to earn a living, to live his life.

Robinson entered the meeting with Rickey remembering a frustrating experience he had had on April 16, 1945. Jackie, together with two other black players—Sam Jethroe, who would one day make the major leagues, and Marvin Williams, who would not—had showed their stuff at Boston's Fenway Park.

Political pressures had forced the tryout. "Nobody put on an exhibition like we did," Robinson recalled. "Everything that we did, it seemed that the good Lord was guiding us. Everything the pitchers threw up became a line drive someplace.''

When the tryout was over, Joe Cronin, Boston manager, claimed he was impressed with the skills shown by Robinson and the other black athletes. "It's too brief a tryout," said Cronin, "to come up with any definite plans, though." The three players were informed that they would possibly be contacted later on; they were handed application forms to complete, and the tryout was over.

Black newspaper reporters attacked the tryout as a "setup." Wendell Smith of the *Pittsburgh Courier* wrote, "Tom Yawkey could have signed all three players for nothing, but he wouldn't take any one of them because they were black."

Two days before the Fenway Park tryout, two other black players had been looked at by the Brooklyn Dodgers. Though they lacked the skills and the youth of the three that were showcased at Fenway Park, black newspaper reporters lumped all five athletes together in their anger at white baseball. "Five black players had auditioned in two days," wrote one reporter, "and the bars are still up. It's the most humiliating experience Negro baseball has yet suffered from white organized baseball."

The anger and the memory of these "tryouts" were in Jackie Robinson's mind as he met with Branch Rickey.

The Brooklyn morning sun was blocked by the drawn venetian blinds. The solidly built Rickey came from behind his desk with his hand outstretched in greeting.

Jackie shakes hands with Branch Rickey upon signing a contract to play for the Brooklyn Dodgers.

—30—

"Jackie Robinson." There was a smile on the older man's face. "It's nice to meet you. I understand you're quite a ballplayer. Please take a seat." Rickey gestured toward a leather chair facing his neat desk. "We have a lot of things to talk about," the executive smiled. "And we've got plenty of time to do it."

Rickey puffed on his cigar. He looked straight at Jackie Robinson, the smoke curling up from the cigar. "The truth is," said the former catcher, getting right to the reason for the meeting, "you are not a candidate for the Brooklyn Brown Dodgers. You were brought here to play for the Brooklyn organization, to start out, if you can make it, playing for our top farm team, the Montreal Royals."

Robinson was shocked by Rickey's words. A frown formed on his face. He mouthed the words slowly: "Me, play for Montreal?"

"Yes." Rickey smiled. "If you can make the grade. Later on . . . you'll have a chance with the Brooklyn Dodgers. I want to win pennants. We have scouted you for weeks. What you have done is a matter of record. But this is much more than just playing baseball, much more. The main question is, do you have the guts to make it?"

"I'll make it if I get the opportunity to make it." Robinson said the words quickly, seizing the opportunity to get out a statement between the long-winded comments of Rickey.

"I know you're a good ballplayer," the older man was off again. He explained that he wished that making the grade in baseball were a matter of pure ability, but then added, "that's not the way it is today, but maybe because of what you will be able to do, the day will come when ability will be all that matters."

There were a series of questions and answers—long questions by Rickey and short answers by Robinson. The Dodger executive was satisfied that Robinson had no written agreement with the Kansas City Monarchs, his team in the

Negro Leagues, that Robinson's difficulties in the service and, in some instances, on the athletic field at UCLA were caused by prejudice against him as a black man.

"I know all about your battles," Rickey said kindly. "I understand the things you have been through. I know all about your fighting spirit. We're going to use all of those qualities."

Rickey rose and moved closer to Robinson, who remained seated on the leather chair in front of the desk. "Have you the guts to play the game? Have you the courage to play no matter what happens?" Rickey's voice was angry, and the kindly and calm look had now gone from his face. He removed the jacket of his three-piece dark suit. "I must have some answers today!"

Almost on top of Robinson now, Rickey used his cigar as a pointer. "You're standing in the batter's box. I'm a beanball pitcher. I hate you. I wing a fast ball at you. It grazes your cap. It sends you jumping back for cover. What do you do?"

"Mr. Rickey, I'd just pick myself up and dig in."

"In a crucial game," Rickey continued, "I smack the ball into the outfield. It's a very close play. You cover second base. I come in. I lunge toward you." Rickey actually lunged at Robinson, swinging his large fist so that it grazed the black man's chin. " 'Get out of my way, you black son of a bitch, you damn black bastard.' Now what do you do?"

Before allowing Robinson to answer, the heavily perspiring Rickey continued his dramatic performance. He was probing like the lawyer he once was.

"You're at shortstop." Rickey was screaming. "I am the runner at first base." Rickey loosened his tie. "I come down to steal a base. I slide. I cut you in the legs with my spikes. I laugh. 'Now you black nigger, how do you like that?' Jackie, what do you do now?"

Angered at Rickey's words, but also aware that the Dodger executive was playing a role, Robinson snapped out:

"Mr. Rickey, what do you want? A coward? What do you want? A ballplayer who is afraid to fight back?"

"I want," the words Rickey used were measured, "a ballplayer with guts enough not to fight back!"

Rickey relit his cigar and mopped his brow. He explained to Robinson how his family had expressed fear that his health would be negatively affected by the strain of attempting to break baseball's color line. He made it clear that what he and Robinson would be attempting would be met with hostility and hatred by many within the baseball establishment.

"There is no way for us to fight our way through this situation," Rickey explained. He walked over to the window and looked out onto the streets of downtown Brooklyn, at the morning sun forming shadows. "There is virtually no group on our side—no umpires, no club owners, maybe a few newspapermen. There will be some fans and players who will be especially hostile. It will be an almost impossible position. But we can win if we can convince everyone that you are not only a great ballplayer but also a great gentleman."

Rickey explained that he had taunted and teased Robinson to test him. "You will hear much worse and go through much more pressure before you are through," he smiled. "I apologize for the crude language and the testing, but you are a pioneer and the whole experiment depends on you and how you hold up."

"I get it." Robinson appreciated what the older man had done, the opportunity he was providing, and the sacrifices they would both be making. "I can do it. I can turn the other cheek for a while."

The meeting ended with Robinson signing a two-paragraph statement—a contract with the Montreal Royals for the 1946 season. He was to receive a $3,500 bonus and a salary of $600 a month.

"Tell no one," Rickey said, "except those closest to you, about what we've done and about the signing. I'll explain it all at the appropriate time, Jackie."

The appropriate time was October 23, 1945. It came after the World Series and before the Dodger players signed their contracts for the 1946 season. The signing was a signal to the players that blacks would in all likelihood be part of the future of the Brooklyn Dodgers. The news of the signing became one of the most dramatic and controversial sports stories in years. Everyone seemed to have an opinion, a different point of view.

The *Sporting News*, the leading baseball newspaper, indicated that it was upset at those who were against Robinson because he was a black man. Then the newspaper discounted Jackie's chances to succeed:. "At twenty-six, Robinson is reported to possess baseball abilities, which, were he white, would make him eligible for a trial with, let us say, the Brooklyn Dodgers' Class B farm at Newport News, if he were six years younger. . . . The war is over. Hundreds of fine players are rushing out of the service and back into the roster of organized baseball. Robinson will conceivably discover that as a twenty-six-year-old shortstop just off the sandlots, the waters of competition in the International League will flow far over his head."

Satchel Paige, fabled star of the Negro Leagues, disagreed with the view of the *Sporting News*. "Jack's the number one professional player," said Paige. "They couldn't have picked a better man."

A star for the Newark Eagles of the Negro Leagues back in 1945, Monte Irvin was delighted with the signing. "There may have been a certain amount of jealousy by some of the black players that Jack had become the one, but we knew that if he made it, the door would swing wide open for all of us."

Willa Mae Walker, Jack's sister, who was three years older than her brother, said: "The family in California was all very happy. But we were frightened, too . . . because we knew there had never been any blacks in organized baseball and some did not want him to play there."

Branch Rickey's motives were questioned by many. Called "The Great White Father" by some newspapers—and much worse by others—the Dodger general manager was especially upset at the remarks of minor-league baseball Commissioner William Bramham. "Father Divine [a religious leader of the time] will have to look to his laurels, for we can expect a Rickey Temple to be in the course of construction in Harlem soon. Whenever I hear a white man, whether he be from the North, South, East, or West, protesting what a friend he is to the Negro race, right then I know the Negro needs a bodyguard. It is those of the carpetbagger stripe of the white race, under the guise of helping but in truth using the Negro for their own selfish interests, who retard the race."

When some of the negative reactions to the signing were reported, Rickey told Robinson: "Not only will you be on trial, but all of black society. You must be a man big enough to bear the cross of martyrdom. You must not fight back. You must turn the other cheek." Rickey's message not only applied to Jackie, but also to himself. He busied himself anticipating problems, not responding to those who opposed what he called the "Noble Experiment."

At Rickey's suggestion, Robinson was away from November 1945 to January 1946. He played winter ball in Venezuela, removed from the houndings of fans and newspaper reporters. Roy Campanella, who, according to Dodger executive Walter O'Malley, was the runner-up choice to be the first to break baseball's color line, was Robinson's teammate.

"We roomed together," recalls the man who went on to become the greatest catcher in Dodger history, "and we had a chance to do a lot of talking and get real close. Jackie would say, 'I just want a chance to play, and I think I can handle the worst of it.' "

In his own words, here is how Jackie Robinson felt at that time on the verge of his breaking the color line in the International League:

I know I am heading for trouble in Florida next March when I must train with Montreal. I don't look for anything physical. I really believe we've gotten beyond that in this country. I know I'll take a terrible tongue beating, though. But I think I can take it. I'm due for a terrible riding from the bench jockeys all around the International League circuit if I am good enough to play with Montreal all summer. I know about the riding white players give one another, and I'm sure it will be much worse for me because I am a Negro. They'll try to upset me, and they'll have plenty of material, but we've got that also in our league, and I am prepared for it. These days keep reminding me of something my mother told me when I was a little kid. She told me that the words they say about you can't hurt you. And when they see that, they'll quit saying them.

"I've had plenty of nasty things said about me from the stands," Robinson continued, "especially in basketball, where you can hear everything they shout. I never let it get to me. I think it made me play better. I'll always remember what my mother taught me, and I think I'll come through.

"I think I am the right man to pick for this test. There is no possible chance that I will flunk it or quit before the end for any other reason than that I am not a good enough ballplayer. . . . That is the only thing I can be mistaken about now."

In the spring of 1946, Jackie Robinson and the Montreal Royals moved north, completing spring training. The troubles Rickey had been concerned about became a reality. Games were canceled in two Southern cities because of laws against racially integrated competition. A city official in Jacksonville, Florida, padlocked the ball park, affecting the playing of a game. One contest between Indianapolis and Montreal was delayed for an hour in De Land, Florida, when officials claimed that work had to be done on the electrical system at the ball park. Rickey fumed, especially since the scheduled game was a day contest.

When friends tried to calm Rickey down and said those things were expected whenever anyone tried a new social experiment, the Dodger general manager snapped, "I signed Jackie Robinson for just one reason . . . to win the pennant. I'd play an elephant with pink horns if he could win the pennant."

Despite the troubles and the bigots, April 18, 1946, opening day of the International League baseball season, finally arrived. It was the first opening day in four years that the United States was at peace.

Mayor Frank Hague of Jersey City had declared the day a holiday. Schoolchildren were given the day off; hundreds of them were in Roosevelt Stadium along with thousands of New Yorkers who had made their own holiday and had journeyed to New Jersey to see Jackie Robinson's debut.

"Run those bases like lightning," Rickey told Robinson in their pregame talk. "I want you to worry the daylights out of those pitchers. Don't be afraid to steal the extra base . . . just go out there and run like the devil and hit like a siege gun."

The hundreds of reporters, the two bands, the standing-room-only crowd that gave him an ovation the first time he appeared on the field—all of these built the pressure as Jackie Robinson took his position at second base for the Montreal Royals as they competed against the Jersey City Giants.

For Robinson, it was the pressure of proving the critics and bigots wrong; it was the pressure of producing for Rachel, his UCLA sweetheart whom he had married, and of producing for Branch Rickey, who had supported him in every move, for his family, for his race.

Robinson ran like the devil and hit like a siege gun. He

powered Montreal to a 14–1 romp over Jersey City. His daring on the basepaths forced Jersey City pitchers to commit two balks. Jackie stole two bases, recorded three singles, cracked a three-run home run. A dominant force in that first game, Robinson's performance delighted his supporters and gained him many fans.

Jackie Robinson of the Montreal Royals probably received more attention than any other minor-league player in the history of baseball. Some of it was open hatred: dugouts with racist players holding up shoeshine kits or black cats, or screaming curses. Some of it was open admiration: special charter trains filled with fans eager to see the black pioneer in action; mobs of autograph seekers anxious to collect Jackie's signature.

By August 1, 1946, with Jackie Robinson triggering the team's winning ways, Montreal was in first place in the International League pennant race—fifteen games in front of its nearest competition. As the season came close to an end, Robinson gave in briefly to all the pressure that had been on him.

"My nerves were pretty ragged," he explained. "Often I couldn't eat and couldn't sleep. I guess I hadn't realized I wanted to make good so badly. I sort of went to pieces."

Under the orders of a doctor, Jackie took himself out of the Montreal lineup to rest. Then, fearful that people would think he was resting to protect his league-leading batting average, Jackie, after recharging himself for just one day, came back to once more lead the Royals.

Jackie finished the season with a league-leading batting average of .349 and a league-leading fielding percentage of .985. He also stole forty bases and the hearts of the fans of Montreal.

The Royals opposed Louisville in the Little World Series and lost two of the three games played in that Southern city. In those contests Robinson received some of the worst treatment he had suffered all during the 1946 season. "Hey, coon," Louisville players and fans screamed at him, "go back to Canada where you belong." A steady stream of racial threats and curses was directed at Robinson, who was also upset at the quota on the number of blacks allowed to attend the games in Louisville.

All the harsh treatment Robinson suffered in Louisville was reported in detail in the Canadian newspapers. When the Royals returned to Montreal for the final three games of the Little World Series, each Louisville player was booed while Robinson was cheered. The Royals won three straight games and the championship.

After the clinching of the Montreal triumph, fans raced out onto the field. They celebrated the moment, lifting Jackie onto their shoulders.

"It was," a reporter wrote the next day, "probably the only time in history that a black man ran from a white mob with love instead of lynching on its mind." There would be more.

Clay Hopper, the Montreal manager, who had not been happy when Branch Rickey assigned Robinson to the Royals and had asked seriously, "Mister Rickey, tell me, do you really think a nigra's a human being?" was now delighted.

In the midst of the Montreal victory celebration, the Southern-born manager approached Robinson. "You're a great ballplayer," said Hopper, "and a fine gentleman. You're the greatest competitor I've ever seen. It's been wonderful having you on my team."

With Jackie Robinson's banner year now behind him, with the statistics in the record book, step four of Branch Rickey's plan—the creation of a favorable press climate—was now in place. The Dodger executive began to work on the fifth and perhaps most delicate step of his six-stage plan—getting the support and cooperation of the black community.

Well aware that more than 60 percent of the players on the major-league rosters of the time were from the South, Rickey was very sensitive to the problems of white prejudice. At the same time, however, he was concerned about the potential problems that might come from too much black enthusiasm. "Mr. Rickey," Rachel Robinson recalls, "allied himself with Jack totally. He tried to operate in a way that he would be able to anticipate all problems."

Typical of Rickey's efforts was a meeting that took place on February 5, 1947, at the Carleton YMCA in Brooklyn with leading black community representatives. Rickey spoke to them about their responsibilities as "leading Negro citizens of this community. . . . We don't want any Negro to add to the burdens of Jackie Robinson," he explained.

"We don't want Negroes to form gala welcoming committees, to form parades to the ball park every night. We don't want Negroes to strut, to wear badges."

Warning the black leaders about all the problems he anticipated for Jackie, all the jealousy that might surface, all the hatred he knew some bigots had, Rickey continued, "We, therefore, don't want premature Jackie Robinson Days or Nights. We don't want Negroes in the stands gambling, drunk, fighting, being arrested. We don't want Jackie wined and dined until he is fat and futile. We don't want what can be another great milestone in the progress of American race relations turned into a national comedy and an ugly tragedy."

There was almost complete agreement with all the things Rickey said; several minutes of applause followed the speech of the sixty-six-year-old baseball executive.

The slogan "Don't Spoil Jackie's Chances" was approved. It was to serve as a self-policing action. Cards were produced with the slogan on it. These cards were placed in barbershops, churches, bars, and restaurants. Group meetings were held. The main points of Rickey's Carleton YMCA speech were repeated over and over again by him and by others at other gatherings. With the backing of the black community, Branch Rickey had accomplished the fifth step of his master plan.

Spring training of 1947 was the time and the setting Rickey had selected to accomplish the final step of his plan—the gaining of acceptance of Jackie Robinson by his Brooklyn Dodger teammates. The Royals trained with the Dodgers in Havana, Cuba, to avoid some of the problems of the year before that had taken place in the American South.

In addition to Robinson, three other black players were placed on the Montreal roster: catcher Roy Campanella and pitchers Roy Partlow and Don Newcombe.

Dr. Dan Dodson, then a New York University professor and a member of the Committee on Unity, an organization formed to ease racial tensions in New York City, recalls the reason for the spring training setup. "The idea was to let the Dodger team have the experience of playing with, against, and among dark-skinned people . . . bring both the Dodgers and the Royals to Brooklyn playing exhibition games along the way and introduce Robinson gradually."

According to Dodson, Rickey thought that when Dodger players saw how skillful an athlete Robinson was, they would really want to have him on their team. "When they see that his skills can put money in their pockets," said Rickey, "they'll wish to have him on the team if for no other reason than a financial one." It did not happen that way!

Instead, there was just the opposite reaction from some of the players on the Dodgers. Shortstop Pee Wee Reese, from Kentucky, went to Branch Rickey and asked to be traded to another team. "My grandfather would turn over in his grave," said Reese, "if he knew I was playing ball with a colored man."

"Don't make a hasty conclusion," Rickey told Reese. "Take some time to think over what you have on your mind.

Try it my way for a couple of weeks. If you still feel this way, then I'll trade you, because if Jackie makes the Dodgers, he's going to play."

A couple of weeks later Reese met with Rickey. "You can trade me if you want, sir," said the Dodger shortstop. "But I've changed my mind. Robinson's not only a great player; he's also a fine gentleman."

Other Dodgers were even more opinionated against Robinson. Catcher Bobby Bragan, pitcher Hugh Casey, and outfielders Carl Furillo and Dixie Walker all stated that they could not and would not play ball on the same team with a black man. They put their objections in the form of a petition.

Outfielder Duke Snider recalls the way it was: "That prejudice was not part of our life in California. When they circulated the petition, I said there was no way that I could sign it. Jack's an idol of mine. The only ones that signed it were the guys who were passing it around."

One by one Rickey dealt with those who objected to Jackie Robinson. His main line to all of them was that they were free to quit baseball if they desired, but that the "Robinson experiment would continue."

Dodger manager Leo Durocher was more forceful. At a midnight meeting of the team, the fiery pilot snapped, "Some guys here are causing trouble. I don't care one bit how you feel. It doesn't mean a thing to me whether the guy Robinson is blue or orange or black or if he is striped up like a zebra. I manage this team. I say he plays. I say he can make all of us rich. I say that if you can't use the dough I'll see to it that you get the hell out of here."

No one quit baseball, but the crucial sixth stage of Rickey's plan, the clamor by Dodger players for Robinson to join the team, never came to be. Rickey was annoyed and frustrated, but he had another plan that he was poised to set in motion.

This plan involved Durocher telling the press that with Robinson on the Dodger roster, the team could win the 1947 pennant. This also never came to be. On April 9, Leo Durocher was suspended from baseball for one year by Commissioner Happy Chandler. The man they called "Leo the Lip" was charged with "conduct unbecoming to baseball." The battling manager had been involved in an assortment of controversial off-the-field headlines.

The Leo Durocher suspension was the page-one sports story of the year for only one day. For on April 10, the next day, Rickey took matters into his own hands. He authorized the distribution of a press release at Ebbets Field: "Brooklyn announces the purchase of the contract of Jack Roosevelt Robinson from Montreal. . . . He will report immediately. Signed Branch Rickey."

The thousands who had picketed and signed petitions outside of Ebbets Field and who had worn the "I'm For Jackie" buttons were thrilled, as was the man they had stood up for.

"It's what I've been waiting for," said Jackie. "Now I can relax. I have a few days before the season opens, and I'll be ready then. The time element in making good won't be a factor anymore. I'm just going to take a cut at the ball every time a good one comes over the plate, try to connect, run as fast as I can, and play the game hard and clean."

FIRST YEAR AS A BROOKLYN DODGER: 1947

4

The blue number 42 was on the back of his white Brooklyn Dodger uniform as Jackie Robinson took up his position at first base at Ebbets Field on April 15, 1947, opening day of the baseball season. There were 26,623 people in attendance on that spring day, and most of them had come to be witnesses to history—the breaking of baseball's color line. Many wore "I'm For Jackie" buttons.

Slapping the ball sharply to shortstop in his first at-bat, Robinson sped down the line at top speed. He was called out by umpire Al Barlick in a very close play. Scowling, Robinson stepped toward Barlick, prepared to protest the call, but then thought better of it and headed back to the dugout. The Rickey-taught lessons of restraint were in operation.

Robinson was retired in his second at-bat on a fly ball to left field. In his last at-bat of the game, he bounced into a double play. Brooklyn defeated Boston, 5–3, and the first of Jackie Robinson's 1,382 major-league games was now a matter of record.

The next morning *New York Times* sportswriter Arthur Daley noted, "The debut of Jackie Robinson was quite un-

Number 42, Jackie Robinson
steps up to bat.

eventful even though he had the unenviable distinction of snuffing out a rally by hitting into a double play. . . . The muscular Negro minds his own business and shrewdly makes no effort to push himself. He speaks quietly and intelligently when spoken to. . . . 'I was nervous in my first play in my first game at Ebbets Field,' he said with his ready grin, 'but nothing has bothered me since.' "

In the seventh inning of the second game he played in as a Dodger, Robinson recorded the first of his 1,518 major-league hits. He bunted the ball cleanly down the third base line; Boston's Bob Elliott was unable to execute a bare-handed attempt to come up with the ball. Jackie had a bunt single.

"The Negro," the *Brooklyn Eagle* observed the next day, "isn't exactly wearing out the ball, but he's under heavy pressure." Rachel Robinson recalls just how heavy the pressure was:

> It was postwar, and we could not get any housing. We did not have much money. We could only afford one room in a hotel in Manhattan. It was tough living in that room, contending with the reporters, making formula for our son, three-month-old Jackie Jr., and hanging the diapers in the bathroom.
>
> Both of us were strangers to the city. We didn't have friends. We had no relatives in New York City. Jackie Jr. caught a cold on opening day when I took him to the ball park. I was worried about the child. I was worried about the experiment of Jack. We could not even go out and eat together. In the back of the hotel, there was a cafeteria on a side street. One of us would mind the baby. The other would go out and eat, and then we'd switch off. I didn't get sitters. I did not want to leave my baby with anyone. I did not miss a game. It was like going to work with

your husband. I held on to Jack. He held on to me. The baby was part of the whole unit. In those first couple of years, my world was the family and the ball park. . . . I was worried about Jack. He still had to win a spot on the team.

Oh, did he win a spot on the team! On April 18, a year to the day he had broken baseball's color line in the International League as a member of the Montreal Royals, Jackie Robinson recorded the first of his 137 career home runs. It was hit at the Polo Grounds as the Dodgers defeated the New York Giants, 10–4. Although it was a home run hit in the park of the Dodgers' arch foes, Robinson received many cheers from the huge Harlem crowd that had come to see him play.

Even that memorable home run was performed under pressure. "The one thing that concerned Jack," Rachel Robinson explains, "was the possibility of an overenthusiastic black response. We saw it more in the South than we saw it in Brooklyn, but every time he came up to bat early on, even if he hit a pop-up, there would be a tremendous response. His concern was that this might lead to fights in the ball park, but it didn't happen." Part of the reason it didn't happen was that Branch Rickey had done so much work, along with community leaders, insisting, "Don't Spoil Jackie's Chances."

In the churches, in the professional organizations, in the restaurants, and in meeting halls, Mal Goode, a black newspaperman of the time, recalls, "The word was passed on. 'If you hear the bad words, ignore them.' This message went from city to city wherever Jackie played. We all knew that if Jackie made good, the door would be opened."

Although hundreds of thousands of Americans were sympathetic to and involved with the "Noble Experiment" of Jackie Robinson, there were others who could not accept the fact that a black man was succeeding in what had always been a white man's game.

Early in the 1947 season Robinson felt the full fury of this prejudice. The Dodgers were playing the Phillies. "Hey, nigger, why don't you go back down South and play with the other coons?" "Blackie, won't you do me a favor and shine my shoes?" The words were shouted from the Philadelphia dugout, allegedly led by Alabama-born Manager Ben Chapman. For two days the hate language was hurled at Robinson; the Dodgers kept silent. Finally, Eddie Stanky, Brooklyn second baseman, spoke out. "You're all a bunch of cowards," screamed the little Alabama-born player. "You know Robinson can't fight back. Why don't you pick on those like me who can give it back to you?" Other Dodgers backed Stanky.

The series concluded, Rickey was disgusted with the abuse Robinson had suffered, but pleased with the way Stanky and other Dodgers had spoken out on behalf of their badgered teammate. "When Chapman and the others poured out that stream of unconscionable abuse," said Rickey, "it solidified and unified thirty men, not one of whom was willing to sit by and see someone kick around a man who had his hands tied behind his back."

An article in the May 9, 1947, edition of the *New York Herald Tribune* related more of the opposition and hatred Robinson had to deal with during his rookie season. Writer Stanley Woodward reported how a strike by the St. Louis Cardinals as a protest to Jackie Robinson being in the Brooklyn Dodger lineup had been prevented. The strike had been planned for May 6, the date of the first 1947 meeting between the Cardinals and Dodgers. Woodward's story said that National League President Ford Frick sent this message to the St. Louis Cardinals:

If you do this, you will be suspended from the league. You will find that the friends that you think you have in the press box will not support you, that you will be outcasts. I do not care if half the league strikes. Those who do it will encounter quick retribution. They will be suspended, and I do not care if it wrecks the National League for five years. This is the United States of America, and one citizen has as much right to play as another. The National League will go down the line with Robinson, whatever the consequence. You will find that if you go through with your intention that you have been guilty of complete madness.

The first on-the-field physical threat to Jackie Robinson took place in a St. Louis-Brooklyn game. Harry "the Cat" Brecheen was the Cardinal pitcher. Robinson nubbed a bouncer between first base and the mound. A nimble athlete, Brecheen broke off the mound and fielded the ball as Robinson sped down the line toward first base. Brecheen did not flip the ball to the first baseman, Stan Musial, for the routine out but loped over to the first-base line. The Cardinal pitcher extended both fists and moved into a half crouch, awaiting Robinson. Angered at Brecheen's tactics, Robinson pulled up and allowed himself to be tagged out. "You better watch out," he raged at the little Cardinal pitcher. "You better play your position as you should. If you ever pull that stunt again, I'll send you right on the seat of your pants."

Duke Snider, Robinson's Dodger teammate, recalls the atmosphere of 1947. "It takes a special type of person like Jackie who can brush off the things done to him. Branch Rickey had to select someone who could take it, and Jackie could take it. I saw base runners go at him in that first year when he was playing first base. They'd try to step on him, try to cut his leg off."

All of the physical and verbal confrontations were part of the "cross of martyrdom" that Rickey had warned Robinson about. Through it all, there was the need for Robinson to control himself, to realize that a race riot could be triggered by violence on the field.

One of the more dangerous physical incidents took place in a game against the Chicago Cubs. The Dodgers were leading in the ninth inning in a game that would give the Wrigley Field team its fourth straight loss. On second base, having singled and then stolen a base, Robinson danced about, bidding for a steal of third. Cub pitcher Bill Lee continually threw the ball to his shortstop Len Merullo, trying to pick off Robinson. Scampering back to second base to avoid the tag, Robinson had to duck under the legs of Merullo. Their bodies became tangled, and the Cub shortstop wound up on top of a prone Robinson. It seemed for a moment as Merullo rose that he was going to kick Robinson. Jackie cocked his left arm in self-defense. The two men separated. There was a lot of staring. There were some harsh words exchanged. Fortunately, the game resumed without any violence.

"Jack," recalls his brother Mack Robinson, "had grown up not being bossed. He could not be bossed. Having been raised in California and having gone to school with a mixed group, Jack had no fear of the white man. He was just used to going out and playing, playing as hard as he could."

Red Barber, back then the "Voice of the Brooklyn Dodgers," remembers the way it was throughout the 1947 season. "It was a sensitive, even delicate situation. And this thing was something you were not suddenly confronted with one day and then didn't have to worry about anymore. It had to be handled inning by inning, game by game, month by month. It was there all the time because when Jackie Robinson came, he came to stay."

The pressure on Robinson was intense on and off the field. There were black cats that appeared from time to time in the dugouts of the opposition. There were the strangely malfunctioning elevators in hotels on the road. There were the restaurants that developed shortages of food when Jackie sat down to order. There were the racial catcalls, the cold stares, the turned backs of bigots.

The other side of the pressure was the attention by curious and adoring fans. In the middle of the 1947 season, when Robinson moved, along with Rachel and Jackie Jr., to a Brooklyn apartment house, the block on which they lived attracted many visitors hoping to catch a glimpse of him. A five-block walk from the subway stop to Ebbets Field became for Robinson a marathon autograph-signing ordeal. Thousands of requests came into the offices of the Brooklyn Dodgers for commercial, social, and charitable appearances by Robinson. Like a Pied Piper, Robinson attracted attention whenever he appeared in public.

"The way things are now," complained an annoyed Branch Rickey, "he's a sideshow. Give him a sporting chance. If I had my way about it, I would place a cordon of police protection around him so that he might be a ball-player."

The pressure of prejudice on the one hand and fan devotion on the other hand did not lessen much during Robinson's rookie year. And he had to balance both, be prepared for both. Gradually, however, with every hit he recorded, with each stolen base, each run scored, each time at bat, his confidence grew. "As he saw he was succeeding on the field," remembers Rachel Robinson, "he began to feel more comfortable."

On the streets of New York City and throughout the United States, many people who had never even had contact with a black man began to openly root for the underdog Robinson. Kids who once used the stance of Stan Musial or Joe DiMaggio now raised their bat high over their right shoulder in imitation of Number 42.

Only once during the 1947 season did Branch Rickey waive his ban on personal appearances by Robinson off the field. It was a special case. Eddie Hamlin, age twelve, had been severely burned when he threw gasoline on a bonfire. Hospital administrators contacted the Dodgers. They said that the boy's idol was Jackie Robinson and that a visit would help the youth's recovery.

Rickey agreed to allow the visit to take place, but it was kept secret from the press and most of the hospital staff. Eddie Hamlin was given an autographed baseball by Robinson and a little speech about fighting back. The youth was discharged from the hospital and was on his way to full recovery a few months later. The news of the Robinson visit was never leaked to the media, even though it would have cast the black pioneer in the most favorable light. Rickey later explained why he acted the way he did. "Judgment of Robinson was to be made by what he did on the baseball diamond and in no other way."

Even Robinson's severest critics had to admit that what he did on the baseball diamond was incomparable. There were times during that 1947 season that the opposition thought he was the team. All the skills and speed that had made it possible for him to excel in basketball, football, track and field, and baseball at UCLA were set in motion. A powerful black man possessed with daring and verve, Jackie Robinson played in one hundred and fifty games in 1947— more than any other Dodger. The league leader in stolen bases, he batted .297.

He was called "Ty Cobb in technicolor." He was a terror for the opponents of the Brooklyn Dodgers. Sometimes he appeared to be an optical illusion. In one game, he scored all the way from first base on a sacrifice by one of his teammates. In another game, he drew a walk and then dashed all the way to second base. His walking leads, his ferocious football-type slides that leveled infielders, his quicksilverlike moves that made it seem as if he were bottled mercury on run-down plays—all of these became part of the Jackie Robinson style and image.

"The ball park was an outlet for his daring," recalls Rachel Robinson. "That was the style that fit well with his personality. Mr. Rickey and the coaches encouraged the full development of that style."

Fans flocked to see him in action. The Dodgers drew 1,807,526 people in 1947, the first of a decade of million-plus seasons with Robinson as the premier attraction. Brooklyn became the team to see as more than two million fans came to watch them in their road games.

Many who were not even baseball fans arranged their lives so that they could take the charter buses, or load up their cars with friends and relatives to see Jackie Robinson play. This was especially true of Southern fans, who would travel long distances to see the "one" who had broken baseball's color line.

"Charter buses used to arrive from all over the South," recalls Jack Lang, a sportswriter who covered the Dodgers. "For a Sunday doubleheader there was always a jammed ball park. The people made it into a festival, a coming together. In the seventh or the eighth inning of the second game, there would be an announcement: 'Bus leaving for Mobile in ten minutes, train leaving for Mobile in twenty minutes.' The park would slowly begin to empty out. Some stayed and missed their train or their bus. They wanted to see Robinson field one more ball, steal one more base, hit one more time."

Near the end of the 1947 season at Ebbets Field, a Jackie Robinson Day was held. Number 42 had proved he belonged. His skills and personality were such that he was one of baseball's biggest drawing cards and in the same class with Joe DiMaggio, Bob Feller, and Ted Williams. Even Branch Rickey felt secure enough to authorize the day in Robinson's honor.

Famed dancer Bill "Bojangles" Robinson was there, along with Jackie's and Rachel's mothers. It was the first time that Mallie Robinson had met Branch Rickey. She thanked him for signing her son and giving him the opportunity to play for the Dodgers. "Don't thank me," smiled the Brooklyn general manager. "If it had not been for you, there wouldn't be any Jackie."

Standing near home plate, Jackie Robinson was moved by the roar of the crowd and the sight of the gifts. "I thank you all," he said over the microphone in that distinctive high-pitched voice. "I especially thank all the members of the Dodgers, who were so cooperative and helpful in helping me improve my game."

The Brooklyn Dodgers won the National League pennant in 1947. The *Sporting News*, which had at one time thought little of Robinson's chances to even make the major leagues, dubbed him their Rookie of the Year. "He was rated solely as a freshman player in the big leagues," said the *Sporting News.* "The award is on the basis of his hitting, his running, his defensive play, his team value."

The Brooklyn Dodgers opposed the New York Yankees on September 30, 1947, in the first game of the World Series. For Jackie Robinson, it was another first—the first time a black man had ever competed in the World Series.

"I was pulling and groaning," Mack Robinson recalls of that 1947 World Series. "I was stretching and grunting on every step and every swing that Jack took. I was playing it all right along with him."

The Yankees, as they were in the habit of doing, won the series. Robinson recorded seven hits to tie Pee Wee Reese for the team lead in hits. He stole two bases. He was flawless in the field. However, his .259 batting average was a disappointment.

"We knew how to pitch to him," remembers Bill Bevens, who almost pitched the first no-hitter in World Series history, only to be racked by Cookie Lavagetto's pinch hit double to give the Dodgers a victory in game three. "We knew he had been a football player, and we felt his shoulders didn't get around that good. We didn't really have any trouble with him. Later on he learned how to hit those pitches."

For the Dodgers and Jackie Robinson and for their fans, the familiar shout of "Wait Till Next Year" went up. "That was a true statement," says former Yankee catcher Yogi Berra. "With Robinson on that team, we knew we'd be facing him and the Dodgers lots of times in the future."

A postscript to the 1947 season is the case of Dixie Walker, the popular Dodger outfielder, who had objected to Robinson's being on the team. Throughout the year Jackie had made it a point to keep away from Walker. "When he hit a home run," Robinson noted, "I made it a priority of mine not to wait at home plate to shake his hand. I thought it would embarrass Walker."

By June of 1947, after seeing what kind of a player and a person Jackie was, Walker became friendly, supportive. "Dixie came to me," Jackie recalled, "and he taught me the trick of hitting behind the runner, something I didn't know much about."

When the season neared its end, Walker announced, "No other player with the possible exception of catcher Bruce Walker did more to put the Dodgers in the race than Jackie Robinson. He is everything that Branch Rickey said he was when he came up from Montreal." Walker went to Branch Rickey and withdrew his request to be traded from the Dodgers.

It was too late. Rickey had traded Walker to Pittsburgh and had obtained pitcher Preacher Roe and third baseman Billy Cox, two men who would perform superbly for Dodger teams in the years ahead.

THE BROOKLYN DODGER DECADE: 1947-1956

5

Jackie Robinson played for the Brooklyn Dodgers for ten years as the dynamo that helped power the team to six pennants and one world championship. Performing under the most intense pressure, with the handicap of being a black pioneer and always seemingly in the middle of one controversy or another, Jackie compiled some very impressive statistics.

For six straight years he batted .300 or better; seven of those ten years as a Dodger he averaged more than a hundred runs scored each season. He played in a total of 1,382 games and recorded 1,518 hits, an average of more than one hit per game. Twice he led the league in stolen bases. A first baseman in 1947, primarily a second baseman from 1948 to 1952, Robinson was so versatile that he played every position except pitcher or catcher through the Brooklyn Dodger decade.

After his historic 1947 season, Robinson spent a lot of time that winter attending banquets and testimonials in his honor. In the words of an observer of that era, "Robinson made the lard circuit." Branch Rickey was very disappointed when Robinson reported to spring training in 1948. He was more than twenty-five pounds overweight, and he was out of shape.

Santo Domingo in the Dominican Republic was the site

of the spring training camp of the Dodgers. Frustrated by the sight of the overweight Robinson, manager Leo Durocher was furious. He made Jackie go through rigorous workouts aimed at getting him in shape. The "Lip" criticized and teased Jackie in front of the press. The confrontations that sprung up between Robinson and Durocher set the stage for a long-range feud between the two men.

Robinson and the Dodgers began the season ineffectively, and on July 16, 1948, partly because of Brooklyn's slow start, partly because of internal politics, Durocher crossed over and became the manager of the New York Giants. Burt Shotton replaced him as Dodger manager.

With Durocher gone, Robinson began to regain his form. The change, as Jackie explained, had nothing to do with Durocher's exit. "It may have seemed to Leo," said Jackie, "that I was goofing off for him and giving all I had for Shotton. It had nothing to do with that. It was just a question of playing myself into shape." Robinson's comments notwithstanding, Durocher was convinced that he had been let down by Jackie.

On the basis of a strong finish, Robinson wound up the 1948 season with a .296 batting average and eighty-five runs batted in. Hit by pitches seven times, he led the league in that category; he was also thrown out of one game, flashing the aggressiveness of the future that would be his trademark. The Dodgers finished the year in third place, seven and one-half games behind the pennant-winning Boston Braves.

The 1949 Brooklyn Dodgers had Robinson, catcher Roy Campanella, who had joined the team the year before, and rookie pitcher Don Newcombe—just three of the blacks from the pipeline of talent that Branch Rickey had tapped into. These players, along with powerful first baseman Gil Hodges, steady shortstop Pee Wee Reese, slick-fielding third baseman Billy Cox, hard-hitting right fielder Carl Furillo, and a young pitching staff, made "Dem Bums" the team to beat in the National League. And with two years of major-league strife and struggle behind him, Robinson was primed to assert himself. Branch Rickey agreed that it was time for Jackie to be his own man.

"I could see how the tensions had built up in him in two years," said Rickey, "and that this young man had come through with courage far beyond what I had asked. I knew also that while the wisest policy for Robinson during those first two years was to turn the other cheek and not fight back, there were many in baseball who would not understand his lack of action. They could be made to respect only the fighting back, the things that are the sign of courage to men who know courage only in its physical sense. So I told Robinson that he was on his own. Then I sat back happily . . . knowing that Robinson was going to show the National League a thing or two."

In spring training of 1949, Robinson issued a challenge through reporters. "They'd better be rough on me," he said, "because I'm going to be rough on them this year." It was a comment on how much in shape he was and how the athlete in him longed for the season to begin. Yet it was misinterpreted by Ford Frick, National League president, who objected to the fierceness of Robinson's comments. Called in for an interview by Frick, Robinson explained that he was no longer going to remain silent in the face of abuse. Jackie explained that he was going to play hard and that if there were threats directed at him by other players he was not going to back down as he had done in the past.

When umpire Al Barlick declared Jackie "out" in the sixth inning of a Dodgers–Giants game, Jackie challenged the decision.

An incident in spring training between Robinson and rookie Dodger pitcher Chris Van Cuyk showed that Jackie meant business. Van Cuyk threw a bit too close to Robinson in a practice game. There was some shouting. The two men almost squared off, but cooler heads prevailed. This incident showcased Robinson's sensitivity, which had developed during his first two seasons as a black pioneer, and his new fiery quality.

Rickey, too, was bolder in 1949. He scheduled a three-game exhibition contest with the Atlanta Crackers prior to the season. The Ku Klux Klan said that there would be marksmen in the stands lying in wait for Robinson. The racist organization issued a statement saying that it was illegal in Georgia for interracial baseball to take place. Robinson came to bat in the first game. It was the first time a man of his race had ever stepped to the plate in a game against the Atlanta Crackers. More than fifty thousand blacks and whites turned out for the three-game series. The blacks spilled out of the segregated section of the stands and stood a dozen deep in the outfield.

No violence of any kind took place. "I wouldn't trade shoes," Robinson said after the three games were concluded, "with any man in the world. I always had the feeling that a sports fan is a sports fan anyplace in America."

As the 1949 season got under way, all over the National League players and sportswriters noticed the new aggressiveness of Jackie Robinson. It was as if he was intent on paying back some of the old debts that he had accumulated in those first two seasons. It was clear to everyone that his days of turning the other cheek were over.

The Dodgers were rolling to a big win over the Phillies one day as Robinson came to bat. "Stick one in his ear," screamed pitcher Schoolboy Rowe from the Philadelphia dugout.

Robinson was upset. "What kind of a thing is that to say

with the score the way it is?'' he asked the Philadelphia catcher. When the Dodgers completed their turn at bat, the catcher told Rowe what Robinson had said.

"You tell him," Rowe said angrily, "if he's got anything to say about it to say it to my face."

At bat again, Robinson heard the catcher repeat Rowe's message. Looking into the Philadelphia dugout, Robinson screamed at Rowe, casting doubt on the veteran pitcher's courage.

Rowe charged out of the dugout, prepared to fight. Robinson stood his ground. Violence was prevented as players from both teams stepped between the two angry men.

That 1949 season saw Number 42 involved in battles on the field and in the international arena. In July, Robinson versus Paul Robeson became a world news story.

Robeson, a noted singer and a former great athlete and a black man, had issued a statement from Paris. His main point was that American Negroes would not fight in a war for the United States against the Soviet Union. Summoned before the House Un-American Activities Committee, Robinson, as a leading black athlete, was asked to testify.

"I can't speak for any fifteen million people any more than any other person can, but I know that I've got too much invested for my wife and my child and myself in the future of this country, and I and other Americans of many races and faiths have too much invested in our country's welfare for any of us to throw it away because of a siren song sung in bass.

"But that doesn't mean that we're going to stop fighting race discrimination in this country until we've got it licked. It means that we're going to fight it all the harder because our stake in the future is so big. We can win our fight without the communists, and we don't want their help."

Years later Robinson expressed a certain degree of regret at taking on Paul Robeson with so much force. "I had much more faith in the ultimate justice of the American white man back then than I have today," he said. But in 1949, just less than three years into his breaking of baseball's color line, it was an appropriate stance for the black pioneer, and it won him much praise in the press.

"True Hero" . . . "The Right Slant" . . . "Jackie Bats .1000 in Probe of Reds" were just a few of the hundreds of newspaper headlines that projected him from baseball star to international celebrity.

Despite his growing fame and public image, Robinson was a man apart, sometimes much misunderstood. "Jack was not a socializer," explains Rachel Robinson. "He was not one to hang out with the boys, or have a beer on the corner. The behavior was often misunderstood as snobbishness. He'd make a beeline for home after a game or to a golf driving range, where he'd go hit some golf balls before dark. That was his way . . . he never expected a fair share from some of the writers. Some of the tension between him and the press was that they wanted to talk about the score; he wanted to talk about social issues."

Former home-run king Ralph Kiner, today a broadcaster for the New York Mets, recalls that 1949 prime year of Jackie Robinson. "He was the only player I ever saw who could completely turn a game around by himself, to hang in there under the worst kind of pressure, to antagonize the opposition to the benefit of his own team."

Powered by Jackie Robinson, the 1949 Dodgers won ninety-seven games and the National League pennant. Robinson won the National League batting title with a .342 average. He paced the league in stolen bases with thirty-seven. Second in hits and runs driven in, Robinson was also third in triples, runs scored, and slugging percentage. He was not only a potent force at bat but also a wizard in the field, leading all National League second basemen in double plays. The performance was more than good enough to earn him the Most Valuable Player award.

Through that Brooklyn Dodger decade, Jackie Robinson was always the team's most valuable player. Game after game, inning after inning, when a clutch hit was needed, a stolen base, a pep talk to a team member, a key fielding play, or a challenge to the opposition—Number 42 was always ready.

One particularly controversial and violent example of Robinson asserting himself took place in a game between the New York Giants and the Brooklyn Dodgers. The two teams, arch rivals for the affection of New York City fans, seemed to always play harder, more competitive baseball against each other than against any other National League teams.

On this particular day in the game played at Ebbets Field, swarthy Sal Maglie pitched for the Giants. A fierce competitor, Maglie had been nicknamed "The Barber" because of his habit of shaving the plate with his pitches and also throwing dangerously close to batters. In this game, Maglie's "barbering" was especially close. He "nicked" a couple of Dodger batters and dared them to dig in at the plate. Reese, the Dodger captain, was concerned about the possibility of injury to his teammates.

"We've got to do something about Maglie," Reese told Robinson. "Somebody's going to get hurt bad unless we give him a lesson. The next time you come up, Jack, bunt down the first-base line. See if you can dump Maglie when he comes over to field the ball."

Robinson dropped a bunt down the first-base line, but the veteran Maglie remained on the mound. First base was covered by Giant second baseman Davey Williams. Robinson sped down the base line and banged into Williams, sending him toppling backward. Running with his head down, Robinson was like a locomotive. He hadn't noticed it was Williams on first base and not Maglie.

"Williams got in the way," Robinson explained later. "He had a chance to get out of the way, but he just stood there right on the base. It was too bad, but I knocked him over. He had a Giant uniform on. That's what happens."

All of the Giants were enraged at what had happened. "It was a cheap shot," recalls Monte Irvin, who played for the Giants back then. "In fact, it nearly ruined Davey Williams's career. Durocher called us all down underneath the dugout. He was furious. He told us that we were going to give it back to Robinson."

A couple of innings later Giant shortstop Alvin Dark pounded the ball into the left-field alley. Dark had an easy stand-up double, but he raced around second base on his way to third base, Robinson's position. Sliding with spikes up intent on "giving it back to Robinson," in Irvin's phrase, Dark came up short. Reese's relay throw was plucked out of the dirt in front of third base by Robinson, who stepped back to avoid Dark's spikes. Robinson tagged the sliding Giant in the nose with the ball. Dark was safe as the ball bounced away. "I would have torn Dark's face up," said Robinson, "for going at me like that. I am glad that it didn't turn out that way. I admired Dark for what he did after I cut down Williams."

Just as he would not back off from confrontation and was loyal almost to a fault to his team, Jackie could also respect players like Dark and others who played all out.

Despite his fierce aggressiveness, Robinson was also a caring colleague of those he played with and in some instances those he played against. "When I was a pitcher for the Dodgers," recalls Ed Roebuck, "I was not really a star. The team had so many stars, and Jackie Robinson was the Brooklyn Dodgers. Yet he made me feel at home. He'd come out to the mound. He knew how I felt. 'C'mon, Ed,' he would say. 'You can do it. You can pitch up here. We all know you can.' "

Others received different treatment, but the motivation was the same. Newcombe was sometimes a target for angry words from Robinson. The huge black Dodger pitcher had a tendency to lose confidence, to get down on himself. "Jackie used to tell me," recalls Newcombe, " 'the only time you pitch good is when you get mad. I'm going to keep you mad.' " Newcombe smiles, "whenever I needed it, he got on me. It helped."

In 1951 twenty-year-old Willie Mays came up to star for the New York Giants. And he, too, like other blacks throughout the National League, received encouragement from Jackie Robinson. The two would talk on the phone at night and the rookie Mays would receive information on how to hit certain pitchers, how to position himself for fielding against different kinds of hitters. None of the information, of course, was about Dodger players—Robinson never went that far.

By 1950, the walk, the look, and the voice of Jackie Robinson were as well known to New Yorkers and baseball fans as were his exceptional playing skills. And he began to gain some financial benefits from athletic efforts.

His rookie season salary with the Dodgers was $5,000. It jumped to nearly $13,000 his second season. By 1950 he was earning $35,000, the highest salary ever given to a Brooklyn Dodger up to that time.

Commercial ventures like Jackie Robinson jackets and caps, and a film version of his life story provided him with some more income. On May 17, 1950, *The Jackie Robinson Story* premiered at the Astor Theater in New York City. Newspaper ads for the film announced:

"They'll shout insults at you . . . they'll come in at you spikes first . . . they'll throw at your head . . . but no matter what happens, you can't fight back. Yes, only in America could a man have the courage, the will, and the greatness to face such overwhelming odds with only a ball . . . a bat . . . and a glove . . . and win. Jackie Robinson—the pride of Brooklyn—as himself."

The pride of Brooklyn, the favorite of fans all over that America of 1950, Robinson, to some bigots, was still a black

man playing in what had always been a white man's game. And they resented him for it. Others went beyond resentment into open threats of violence.

A letter was sent to the Dodgers, the Cincinnati Reds, a newspaper in Cincinnati, and that city's main police headquarters. The letter warned that when Robinson came to Cincinnati he would be shot. It explained that a gunman would be positioned in one of the buildings that overlooked Cincinnati's ball park, Crosley Field.

Massive security was on hand as the Dodgers came to the ball park. FBI agents spent time with Robinson prior to the game advising him about their safety precautions, attempting to reassure him. Police roamed about throughout Crosley Field and in the nearby buildings, searching for a sniper.

Dodger outfielder Gene Hermanski, after the FBI agents had left the tense Robinson, attempted to lessen the threatening atmosphere. "All of us," he smiled to his teammates, "should wear number 42. We'll be able to protect Robby that way."

"Now if you'd brought along a little soot to paint yourself black and practiced walking pigeon-toed," Robinson joked, "you'd be able to wear number 42 and be of some help."

In Crosley Field, thousands of blacks were in the stands. Many of them had come from Southern cities and had traveled long distances to view Robinson in action, and catcher Roy Campanella (who joined the Dodgers in 1948) and pitcher Don Newcombe (who joined the Dodgers in 1949). In addi-

This letter was sent to Warren Giles,
president of the Cincinnati Reds,
threatening to kill Jackie Robinson
if he played for the Dodgers
at Crosley Field in Cincinnati.

tion to its fears about the possible threat to Robinson's life and to the lives of the other black players, the FBI was also aware of the potential violence that might follow an assassination attempt.

A Jackie Robinson home run gave the Dodgers a win the first game of a scheduled doubleheader. The ball that he hit landed in the vicinity where an assassin might have been positioned. Crossing home plate after running out the home run, Jackie shook hands with outfielder Cal Abrams, who had been the base runner when Robinson hammered the home run.

"My God, Jack," wisecracked Abrams, "let's not stand out here in full view of everyone. Let's get into the dugout quick," said the Jewish outfielder. "If they are ever gonna shoot the two of us, now's the time."

The time never came; the Dodgers played their games in Cincinnati without incident and moved on to the next National League city. However, the hate letter signed by the "Three Travelers" that threatened the assassination of Jackie Robinson was just one of the many pressures the man who broke baseball's color line had to contend with throughout his Brooklyn Dodger decade.

Number 42 had another banner year in 1950. His .328 batting average was second best in the National League. He led all second basemen in double plays and fielding percentage. Yet the year was a major disappointment for him and the fans of the Brooklyn Dodgers. For on the last day of the season, Dick Sisler of Philadelphia slammed a three-run home run to defeat the Dodgers and win the pennant for the Phillies.

"I won't ever forget that moment in my life," Sisler recalls. "We had to win the game or else we would've gone into a play-off. I don't think we would've won the play-off. Our pitching was shot. The pitch was a high fast ball. I put the wood to it. I didn't know it was gone until I rounded first base."

The frustrating loss to the Phillies made Robinson very upset, but a greater loss for him was yet to be. On October 26, 1950, after months of behind-the-scenes power struggles, Walter O'Malley won his battle and eased out Branch Rickey as Dodger general manager and president. "The whole thing was a matter of finances and ego," recalls Stan Lomax, a radio announcer of that era. "They were two dynamic people in one organization. You can only have one. It turned out that it had to be O'Malley."

The last general manager the Dodgers ever had, Rickey moved on to build a third National League powerhouse in Pittsburgh. And Robinson was left without his confidant and beloved friend.

Many of Rickey's aides were fired; negative feelings about him were expressed under the new Dodger regime. Robinson, loyal to Rickey, was upset about some of the things being said about him and defended the man they called "The Mahatma." O'Malley did not like this.

"I will always defend Mr. Rickey," Robinson said. "I owe him a debt of gratitude. I will always speak out with the utmost praise for the man." Robinson's stand caused strained relations. "I never had any difficulties with the Dodger organization," Jackie later recalled, "until Branch Rickey left."

One of the difficulties came because of Robinson's stands on the bombing of churches in the Miami area, triggered by the ruling of the Supreme Court that banned segregation in schools. Robinson condemned the bombings. O'Malley said it was not a fit subject for a member of the Brooklyn Dodgers to get involved with.

"I was not O'Malley's kind of black," said Robinson. "Campanella was." The popular Dodger catcher maintained that perhaps the trouble in Miami was caused by blacks who wanted too much, too fast. "I always thought being up in the major leagues was like being in heaven," said Campanella. "I didn't complain. Jackie was a politician, wanted to be a politician. I didn't. I would exercise my vote and urge all blacks to exercise their vote, but I'd be darned if I'd get up on a soapbox and preach."

Monte Irvin, now in the Hall of Fame, who played against Robinson and who was one of the top performers of the golden age of New York City baseball in the 1940s and 1950s, recalls how he viewed the public stands of Jackie: "There were those who did not appreciate his outspoken views. We thought Jackie was putting himself into situations where he shouldn't have been. He was not a politician. He was not a spokesman for anybody. He was assuming that role. Since he was the first, maybe he thought he had the responsibility, but most of the black players thought he was setting himself up as a spokesman for the entire Negro race."

Outspoken, a crusader, a troublemaker—these were the words some used to describe the new militancy of Jackie Robinson on and off the field as the United States moved through struggles in housing, education, and integration of the 1950s. "I have a right to my opinions," Robinson replied. "I'm a human being. I have a right to fight back."

Since he was the first, the black pioneer, there were always those ready to find fault with him, those always ready to say he was too aggressive. However, there were also many who supported him totally and understood the motivations behind his behavior.

"If some didn't like Jackie," recalls his former white Dodger teammate Ben Wade, "it was for no other reason than he was black. He said some things I didn't like, some tough things, did some tough things, but he had a right, he earned the right."

Irvin and Robinson, of the New York Giants and the Brooklyn Dodgers, had a cat-and-mouse struggle throughout the 1951 season for the pennant. On the last day of the season, they were tied for first place. The Dodgers opposed the Phillies, the club that had beaten them in 1950, on the final day of the season to win the pennant. The Giants played their last game of the regular season against the Boston Braves.

Trailing 8–5 in the seventh inning against the Phillies, the Dodgers received the news that the Giants had defeated the Braves, 3–2, for their seventh straight triumph. The win ensured that the Giants had at least tied for the pennant.

Scoring three times in the eighth inning, the Dodgers tied up their game, 8–8. "What would happen later," Rachel Robinson recalls, "would always rank as one of Jack's biggest thrills in baseball."

Sunday blue laws banned the turning on of the lights in Philadelphia as the two teams played into extra innings, tied 8–8, before more than thirty thousand excited fans.

In the bottom of the twelfth inning, with Philadelphia pitcher Robin Roberts on third base, Eddie Waitkus slugged a low line drive over second base. Robinson broke for the ball, lunged, caught it, and bellyflopped to the ground. His elbows were forced into his chest, and he blacked out for a couple of moments, but somehow he managed to hold on to the ball to record the out and deny Philadelphia victory on that play.

"I touched home on that play," Robin Roberts recalls, 'and I thought the game was over. I still think he trapped the ball, but the umpire said that he caught it. I still wonder."

Bruised and shaken, Robinson remained in the game as it moved on through the descending Philadelphia dusk. In the top of the fourteenth inning, Robinson came to bat. There were two outs. Making contact with full force, he slammed a Roberts pitch high and deep into the left-field stands. The home run gave the Dodgers a 9–8 triumph. His Brooklyn teammates lined up at home plate as Robinson came in to score. They lifted him onto their shoulders and readied themselves for the second play-off in National League history.

Robinson had played for Montreal back in 1946 when the Dodgers and Cardinals battled in the first National League play-off.

The game-saving catch of the Waitkus line drive and the game-winning home run capped Robinson's 1951 season. It was a year in which he batted .338 (third best in the league) and recorded thirty-three doubles—his fifth straight year of thirty or more two-base hits. He paced all second basemen in fielding percentage, putouts, assists, and double plays.

Playing on the first two days of October 1951, the Giants and Dodgers split the first two play-off games. The season came down to game three on October 3, 1951, at the Polo Grounds amidst a carnival-type setting and overcast skies. The pitching match-up was burly Don Newcombe of the Dodgers against crafty Sal Maglie of the Giants.

Robinson's single in the first inning, following walks to Reese and Duke Snider, staked the Dodgers to a 1–0 lead. In the bottom of the seventh inning, the Giants tied the score.

Sitting on the Dodger bench as the top of the eighth inning got under way, Newcombe claimed he was exhausted, that he could not pitch anymore. "Don't give us any of that," Robinson yelled at Newcombe. "You get out there next inning and pitch. We can win this game!"

The Dodgers scored three times in the top of the eighth. The lead and Robinson's pep talk seemed to have a positive effect on the man they called "Newk." He struck out all three batters he faced in the bottom of the eighth.

In the bottom of the ninth, Newcombe was spent. The Giants had one run in and runners on second and third base

Brooklyn teammates rise from their Polo Grounds dugout to congratulate Jackie after he hits a homer.

when Ralph Branca came in to replace him on the mound for the Dodgers.

The home run hit by Bobby Thomson at 3:58 P.M. over the wall in left field at the Polo Grounds has taken on the quality of a legend. Dubbed the "Shot Heard 'Round the World," Thomson's three-run blast gave the Giants an incredible come-from-behind triumph and stunned everyone at the Polo Grounds.

Pandemonium prevailed; some fans cried, others cheered, and others were hypnotized by the sight of Thomson running out the home run. Only Jackie Robinson remained at his position in the field. He carefully studied Thomson's every move, checking to see that the Giant touched each base. Hands on hips, a disappointed, hurt look on his face, Robinson hated to lose. "What he did," explains Rachel Robinson, noting the tumult of that time, "was so characteristic of him. He knew the rules. He knew every part of the game. It was typical of his need to win."

In 1952, with the memory of pennant-denying losses in the last games they played in 1950 and 1951 still with them, the Dodgers of Brooklyn posted a record of ninety-six wins and just fifty-seven losses. They finished four and a half games ahead of the Giants and won the pennant.

Robinson tied his career season high of nineteen home runs. He stole twenty-four bases. He batted .308. He also led all National League second basemen in double plays.

For the fans of the Dodgers, 1952 snapped the last-day-of-the-season jinx that had knocked them out of two World Series; yet now in the fall classic, "Dem Bums" still had another jinx to contend with—how to defeat the New York Yankees.

The series ran seven games, and when it was over, the Bronx Bombers had another world championship banner; the Dodgers had another case of bitter frustration. For Robinson, who managed just four hits in twenty-three at-bats, it was a particularly frustrating series.

As the 1953 season began, Robinson was able to take some satisfaction in the fact that there were seven teams in the major leagues who had black players on their rosters, that there were, in all, twenty-three blacks in the majors. And though he and his Dodger teammates had been stymied in 1947, 1949, and 1952, in their attempts to defeat the New York Yankees in the World Series, 1953 was another year.

The 1953 Dodgers romped to a 105–49 record and the National League pennant. Jackie Robinson batted .329 and ached for the opportunity to once again meet the Yankees in the World Series. Once again the Bronx Bombers prevailed, this time in six games. Robinson made up for his dismal showing in 1952. He batted .320 in the 1953 series, recording eight hits in twenty-five at-bats, including two doubles.

Casey Stengel's 1953 New York Yankees set a new World Series record—five consecutive championships. The Dodgers and their fans were left with the familiar cry of "Wait Till Next Year." Next year for Charlie Dressen, who had succeeded Burt Shotton, never came as Dodger manager.

The man who was Jackie Robinson's favorite manager demanded a two-year contract from the Dodgers after the 1953 World Series. He bragged that he had won two straight pennants; two hundred ninety-eight games in three seasons for a .642 percentage. He reasoned that he had a better record than Leo Durocher, and "The Lip" had just signed a contract for three years with the Giants. Walter O'Malley, Dodger owner, listened to the arguments, and then replaced the outgoing Dressen with the conservative, defensive Walter Alston.

Dressen viewed Robinson as his star of stars. "Give me nine guys like Jackie Robinson," the bubbly manager was fond of saying, "and I'll never lose." Alston viewed Robinson as just another valuable member of the skilled Dodger team. He also thought that Jackie was a bit too assertive.

The personality differences that split Alston and Robinson were symbolized by a 1954 game played at Wrigley

Field. Duke Snider hit a ball into the left-field stands. It came back onto the playing field. Umpire Bill Stewart claimed that the ball hit the wall; Robinson, raging, claimed that a fan had touched the ball. He argued that Snider should have been credited with a home run. Alston was furious that Robinson had raced out on the field to argue with the umpires, but he stood silent in the third base coaching box, taking no part in Robinson's protest.

When the game ended, Alston complained to some of the Dodgers about "Jackie's temper tantrum." Robinson was informed of the Brooklyn manager's comments.

"The team might be going somewhere," was Robinson's response, "if Alston had not been standing on the third base line like a wooden Indian. The run meant something in a close game like that, so whether I was right or wrong, it paid to protest to the umpire . . . but not according to Alston. What kind of a manager is that?"

A photograph in the newspaper the next day made clear that a fan had indeed touched the ball and that Robinson's protest had been proper. Next to the photograph was a story that carried the "wooden Indian" comment about Alston. Both served to anger Alston.

The 1954 Dodgers finished in second place, five games behind the pennant-winning New York Giants. Alternated between third base and the outfield, Robinson batted .311 and played in one hundred thirty-six games, his lowest total to that point in his career as a Dodger.

In spring training of 1955, Alston used Robinson sparingly. Jackie became edgy about his role on the team. He attempted to find out from a sportswriter what Alston's plans were. At a team meeting Alston attacked Dodgers who went to the press to discuss the team; Robinson attacked managers who didn't communicate better with their players. The two strong men were prevented from coming to blows when muscular Gil Hodges grabbed Robinson. "Take it easy, Jackie," he smiled. "It's something not worth fighting about. Take it out on the other teams."

The Dodgers did take it out on other teams in 1955, but Robinson was a shadow of his former self. The "Bums" paced the National League in stolen bases, homers, runs scored, batting average, and slugging percentage; Brooklyn pitchers had the most saves and strikeouts in the league and the lowest staff earned-run average. It was a potent collection of talent that finished thirteen and one-half games ahead of second-place Milwaukee.

For Robinson and the Dodgers, meeting the Yankees in the World Series was like repeating a nightmare. In 1947, 1949, 1952, and 1953, the two teams had met, and each time the Bronx Bombers had been victorious. Although Jackie had missed almost a third of the Dodger games during 1955, had driven in just thirty-six runs and had managed just sixteen extra base hits, he ached to compete against the Yankees and to end the jinx the Bronx Bombers seemed to have over the "Bums."

The first game of the series was played on September 28. In the top of the eighth inning, the Dodgers trailed, 6–4. With two outs, Robinson was the runner at third base. Reporters and even fellow ball players had started to call him "the old gray fat man," and he did fit the description as he took his lead off third down the line to home plate. His hair was gray. His body was broad. He had a paunch around his middle.

Whitey Ford pitched the ball to Yogi Berra squatting behind the plate, and Robinson took off. His slide kicked up dust, and the umpire ruled him safe. He had stolen home. Berra and the Yankees protested, but it did them little good. "I took off," Robinson said later. "I didn't care whether I made it or not. I was just so tired of waiting."

The Yankees won that first game of the series, 6–5. They won the second game of the series. Many fans of the Brook-

lyn Dodgers moaned. They began to think that the Yankee domination of the "Bums" was being repeated.

The teams moved to Ebbets Field, home of the Dodgers, for game three. Robinson singled, with the score tied, 2–2. Jumping back and forth in his lead off first base, with Sandy Amoros at bat, Robinson caused Yankee pitcher Bob Turley to lose his concentration and hit Amoros with a pitch. Dodger pitcher Johnny Podres was the next batter.

Behind Turley, at second base, Robinson bluffed and bluffed again a steal of third base. Podres bunted and sped to first base—safe. The bases were loaded with Dodgers.

Ebbets Field rocked with Dodger fans screaming out encouragement for their team. The vaunted Yankee machine was not running smoothly. Turley and the Yankees were well aware of the danger posed by Robinson at third base. Berra still could not get the image of the steal of home in game one out of his mind.

With Jim Gilliam at bat, Robinson went into his act. He bluffed and shuffled, back and forth off third base, leaning toward home plate. "Concentrate on pitching," Berra screamed at Turley, who appeared upset by Robinson's darting, dashing moves. Turley not only appeared upset—he was upset into walking Gilliam on four straight pitches. Robinson crossed the plate, giving the Dodgers a 3–2 lead. There were those who thought they saw Robinson give Turley a big smile in acknowledgment of the "gift run."

The game moved to the bottom of the seventh inning, with the Dodgers leading, 6–3. In that little bandbox of a ball

In the opening game of the 1955 World Series, Jackie steals home in the eighth inning, as Yankee catcher Yogi Berra attempts to tag him.

park, a three-run lead, especially against Yankee power, was not the most comfortable of cushions.

Robinson slapped a pitch by Tom Sturdivant off the left-field screen. Moving with surprising speed, Robby streaked into second base as Elston Howard made a clean play on the ball off the screen. Robinson made a wide turn past second and then seemingly was headed back to second base. Howard fired the ball toward second base, attempting to double off Robinson, but Jackie took off for third base, just beating the throw of relay man Billy Martin. A Sandy Amoros single scored Robinson.

It was a small incident in a ten-year career, taking the extra base on Elston Howard, but it underscored what Leo Durocher had once said of Robinson. "He comes to beat you," marveled Leo. "He comes to win."

After the Dodgers had sealed their 8–3 triumph over the Yankees, Robinson explained his daring base running to reporters. "The way Howard fielded the ball, I knew he would go through with his intention to throw to second base. So I took off. If the regular left fielder for the Yankees, Irv Noren, was out there, I would've held up, because Noren could pretend to throw to one base and actually throw to another. I had to slide. A couple of years ago no slide would have been necessary. However," Robinson smiled, "that was quite a burst of speed by a gray, fat man, wasn't it?"

On October 4, 1955, Johnny Podres of the Dodgers took the mound against the New York Yankees, who tabbed Tommy Byrne as their starting pitcher. The series was tied at three games each.

Podres had been a fifteen-year-old schoolboy living in Witherbee, New York, when Robinson had shattered baseball's color line in 1947. Byrne was born the same year as Robinson, 1919, and had completed his best year in the majors, winning sixteen games against just five losses, to pace the American League in percentage.

Byrne lasted five innings plus. Podres went all the way until 3:43 P.M., when Howard hit a ground ball to Pee Wee Reese, who tossed to Hodges for the final out, giving the Dodgers a 2–0 victory, capping the first and only world championship in Brooklyn Dodger history.

"You had to pinch yourself," recalls Duke Snider. "We were delirious. We finally had done it." Brooklyn celebrated wildly for days and days. Podres and Sandy Amoros, who had made a spectacular catch of a drive hit by Yogi Berra to save the seventh-game victory, and Snider and Campanella and Hodges—those were the names given the most press coverage. Yet Robinson, who batted a puny .182, four hits in twenty-two at-bats, had made his contribution. He scored five runs and acted as cheerleader and role model for his Dodger teammates. He didn't give up.

In 1956 Robinson played on, but the flash and fire and verve were muted. He performed at third base, second base, first base, and even two games in the outfield. He was more a utility player, occasionally given to moments of high performance. Overall, he was winding down, but there were still times in that 1956 season that he was wound up. Duke Snider remembers one special moment in a game at Wrigley Field against the Cubs. The score was tied, 2–2, in the top of the ninth inning. Cub pitcher Sam Jones hit Robinson with a pitch and put him on base.

"Jackie is dancing around and yelling," recalls Snider, "and Sam keeps throwing over to first and yelling louder. Sam gets so mad he throws the ball right at Jackie, who ducks. The ball sails down to the bullpen in the right-field corner. Jackie goes all the way to third. Sam is fit to be tied. Jackie is still yelling and laughing and dancing up the line.

" 'Sam, you've got no guts,' Jackie screams. 'Sam, I'm gonna beat you.' Jackie is infuriating Jones. Well, Sam is looking at Jackie and cursing at him and paying him more attention than the batter, and he throws the next pitch into the dirt. It's just a short passed ball, but here comes Jackie charging down the line and sliding, and the score is three to two, Brooklyn, and we win another. Yeah, after all those years, that Jackie was somethin' else.''

On December 13, 1956, just two months after playing in the last World Series in Brooklyn Dodger history, Robinson, like Ebbets Field two months before, was sold. The ball park of the Dodgers was purchased by a real-estate developer as Dodger owner Walter O'Malley prepared the way for the exodus of the Dodgers to Los Angeles. Robinson was sold for $35,000 to the New York Giants.

According to Robinson's sister Willa Mae, ''From the moment he came to the major leagues, he never stopped looking for other employment opportunities. He never knew if he was going to make it at first and how long it was going to last. But one thing was certain—Jack had made up his mind that 1956 was going to be his last year in baseball.''

Much excitement was created by the sale of Robinson to the Giants, but he never reported to the team that through all his playing years was the main rival of the Brooklyn Dodgers. In January of 1957, he announced his official retirement from baseball in an article in a national magazine.

Giant owner Horace Stoneham, according to reports, offered Robinson a blank check to sign with his team. He dreamed of the financial rewards that would be gained with Jackie and Willie Mays on the same club. ''It would be unfair to the Giants and their fans to take their money,'' said Rob-

Jackie Robinson, thirty-seven years old, announces his retirement from baseball. With him are his wife, Rachel, and their children, David, Jackie, Jr., and Sharon.

inson. "It is a team that needs youth and rebuilding. It does not need me."

Rachel Robinson explains that her husband had looked for a way out of baseball for the final two years of his career. The strain of getting in shape, of playing with the old fire, had become chores. Additionally, "Jack was a person of extreme loyalty," recalls Rachel Robinson. "He had always made up his mind that he would never play for any team but the Dodgers."

In 1957 the Dodgers of Brooklyn played out their last season as a team and moved on to become the Los Angeles Dodgers, and a new image. For many fans of the team, their love affair with baseball ended when the Dodgers left Brooklyn. For millions, in their mind's eye, the memory of Jack Roosevelt Robinson, Number 42, Brooklyn Dodger, remains to this day.

POSTPLAYING CAREER

6

He was out of baseball and was still only in his late thirties. But the image of Jackie Robinson changed from athlete to gray-haired man, a bit heavyset, always neatly dressed in business suits.

There was the additional complication of his diabetes, allegedly discovered during the first or second week after retirement. Robinson took injections for it; he coped with the diabetes as he had coped with the loneliness, the prejudice, the tough times of his major-league career. And he became a vice-president for community relations for Chock Full O'Nuts and was a role model for all who were employed there.

Now there was more time for family matters; there was more time to get involved in social and political issues. Jack, Rachel, and their three children were comfortably settled in a twelve-room house in Stamford, Connecticut. Mrs. Robinson returned to college and was awarded a degree in psychiatric nursing. Jack Jr., Sharon, and David moved through their growing up school years.

Just how much baseball was behind Jackie Robinson is revealed by former St. Louis Cardinal great Red Schoendienst. "I met him on a Manhattan Street," recalls Schoendienst, "and he told me that he did not miss the game one bit. That really surprised me, knowing the force with which he had played."

Even when the wrecker's ball destroyed Ebbets Field, Robinson showed his postcareer change of stance. "I don't feel any loss," he said. "They need those apartments more than they need a monument to baseball."

As the disruptive decade of the 1960s began, Robinson was just forty-one years old. His main concern during those years of social upheaval was what had always been for him a timeless issue—race.

"There are many of us," he said, "who attain what we want and forget those who help us along the line. We say, 'Why should I jeopardize my position? Why should I slip back?' We've got to remember that there are so many others to pull along the way. The further they go, the further we all go."

With these words operating as his personal creed, Robinson gave many hours of time to the Harlem YMCA. He became involved with the Freedom National Bank, an organization founded to promote black capitalism.

He became more and more involved in politics, thinking this was one of the best methods available to influence social change. He approved of Senator Hubert Humphrey's civil rights record and campaigned for him in the Democratic primary of 1960. When Humphrey lost to then Senator John F. Kennedy, a meeting was set up between Robinson and Kennedy. It did not go as well as many had expected. "He couldn't or wouldn't look me straight in the eye," Robinson said of the Democratic candidate.

Richard M. Nixon, Republican presidential candidate, had a good civil rights record, according to Robinson. Additionally, Nixon's running mate Henry Cabot Lodge promised appointment of a black to the president's cabinet.

When Robinson supported Richard Nixon for president over John Kennedy, there was much surprise and criticism from civil rights groups. Robinson felt it was important to support the Republican party. His argument was that he was

*Jackie and ex-heavyweight champion
Floyd Patterson board a plane for
Birmingham, Alabama, in May 1963 to
participate in civil rights demonstrations.*

*Jackie examines the wreckage
of the home of the Reverend A. D. King
in Birmingham. The structure was
bombed by unknown persons.*

doing his part to keep the GOP from going completely "white." This was his way, he explained, of ensuring black representation in both major political parties in the U.S.

Nixon's failure to become involved when civil rights leader Martin Luther King, Jr., was jailed in Georgia for a minor traffic violation must have disappointed Robinson. Even though Kennedy did act on King's behalf, Robinson did not switch his support to the Democratic candidate.

Robinson greatly admired King; yet he differed with the black leader's approach. "As much as I loved him," said Robinson, "I would never have made a good soldier in Martin's army. My reflexes aren't conditioned to accept nonviolence in the face of violence-provoking attacks."

The other side of the coin was the public struggle between Robinson and black leader Malcolm X. Robinson defended United Nations Undersecretary Ralph Bunche against an attack from Malcolm X, who claimed that the black diplomat was being "muzzled by white bosses." Malcolm X counterattacked, implying that Robinson also was a tool of white bosses. "I do nothing to please white bosses," said Robinson, "or black agitators, unless they are things that please me."

In 1962, induction into baseball's Hall of Fame was a cause for celebration for Robinson and for millions of his fans. At the Cooperstown ceremony Robinson called on three members of the audience to stand next to him: his mother, Mallie; his wife, Rachel; and his mentor, ally and friend, Branch Rickey. It was one of the final times the two men would be together.

The Hall of Fame plaque reads:

JACK ROOSEVELT ROBINSON

Brooklyn N.L. 1947 to 1956.
Leading N.L. batter in 1949.

Holds fielding mark for second baseman
playing 150 or more games with .992.
Led N.L. in stolen bases in 1947 and 1949.
Most Valuable Player in 1949.
Lifetime batting average .311.
Joint record holder for most double plays
by second baseman, 137 in 1951.
Led second basemen in double plays 1949–50–51–52.

On December 9, 1965, just eleven days before what would have been his eighty-fourth birthday, Branch Rickey died. He had suffered a heart attack less than a month before and had lingered on in the intensive care unit at Boone County Memorial Hospital in Kansas City until his death.

"The passing of Mr. Rickey," Jackie Robinson told the press, "is like losing a father. My wife and I feel we've lost someone very dear to us. Mr. Rickey's death is a great loss not only to baseball, but to America. His life was full, and I'm sure there are no regrets as far as fulfillment in life. I think he did it all."

Strangely, few blacks were present at the funeral of the man who declined public honors for enabling Jackie Robinson to break baseball's color line. "To accept honors and public applause for signing a superlative ballplayer, I would be ashamed," Rickey had always said.

Jackie Robinson was ashamed at the skimpy turnout of black players. "Not even flowers or telegrams," he said angrily, "and they're earning all that money."

Some people explained the small turnout of black ballplayers as short memory. Others, like Hall-of-Famer Monte Irvin, felt "the warm feeling for Branch Rickey had worn thin. Seemingly since Jack had acted the way he did, been so outspoken and alienated a lot of people, they might have associated Jack's arrogance with his relationship with Branch."

Jackie is inducted into baseball's Hall of Fame.
With him are Branch Rickey, Rachel Robinson,
and Jackie's mother, Mallie.

Just three years after Branch Rickey died, another, even closer figure in the life of Jackie Robinson passed away. His mother Mallie became seriously ill in Pasadena. Notified by phone, Jack flew out to California, but she died before he arrived.

Without Rickey, without his mother, Jackie pressed on, becoming more involved with social and political causes.

On June 17, 1971, twenty-four-year-old Jackie Robinson, Jr., who looked so much like his father and walked with the same pigeon-toed walk, was killed in an automobile accident. He had been driving his brother David's car on the way home to the Robinson house in Connecticut when the accident occurred.

Three years before, Jackie Jr. had been arrested for possession of drugs. It was reported that he had become addicted when he was wounded during active service in Vietnam. Fully cured of his addiction, Jackie Jr. was devoting himself to helping young drug addicts when he was killed.

"You don't know what it's like to lose a son, find him, and lose him again," said the saddened Jackie Robinson. "I guess I had more of an effect on other people's kids than I did on my own. I thought my family was secure, so I went running around everyplace else."

The following year, Jackie Robinson appeared at Dodger Stadium in Los Angeles. He was reunited with some of his former teammates; he had the opportunity to visit and reminisce with family members in Pasadena.

Now a shell of his former physical self, Robinson shocked those who had known him in his prime by his deteriorated condition.

Immobile in his wheelchair as a result of a crippling accident, Roy Campanella recalled the time. "Life twists things about a lot. I was there in a wheelchair, and Jackie was hardly able to see."

His brother Mack remembers the time at Dodger Stadium: "Jack's sight was bad . . . he could no longer drive a car because he was going blind. I was shocked. I did not know his condition was that far gone. I was on the field with him when some fellow threw a baseball to him out of the stands wanting him to autograph it. The ball bounced off the top of his head because he couldn't even see the ball coming. He got a terrific headache from that, and I guess it bothered him a lot to have the public see how much he had deteriorated."

Deterioration continued. There was bleeding from behind his eyes. Efforts to correct it met with little success.

In October of 1972, almost twenty-seven years to the day after he had signed a contract that would break baseball's color line, Jackie Robinson was still persisting, still attempting to break new ground. His hair was pure gray. His once-powerful body was ravaged by diabetes and leg ailments. He attended the 1972 World Series in Cincinnati in October and was interviewed over national television. "I'd like to live to see a black manager," he said with the old force. "I'd like to live to see the day when there is a black man coaching at third base."

Such statements attracted attention and controversy. To those who criticized him for using the World Series as a forum for his views, Robinson answered, "What better place? What better time?"

Jack Roosevelt Robinson's time ran out at 7:10 A.M. on October 24, 1972, nine days after his appearance at River-

*Jackie signs autographs before
the start of the "Oldtimers" game
in Anaheim, California, in 1969.*

front Stadium in Cincinnati. He collapsed in his Stamford home. Police gave him oxygen and applied external massage. He was sped to the Stamford Hospital by fire department ambulance. Nothing helped.

Jackie Robinson was fifty-three years old at the time of his death. All kinds of speculation has been advanced about his untimely death—the stresses of his life, the diabetes, the death of his son, the pressures of his early years in baseball as a black pioneer.

"Jack didn't die of heartbreak," says Rachel Robinson, the one person closest to him. "He didn't die of pressure. He died of a very virulent disease that may have been advanced by the stress."

The news of the death of Jackie Robinson affected millions, for he touched millions with his brilliant style of play on the baseball field, with his image as a fighter against tremendous odds. There were more than twenty-five hundred people in the congregation at Riverside Church at his funeral on October 27, 1972. The coffin was covered with red roses. The Reverend Jesse Jackson delivered the eulogy as the famous and the ordinary people, who had come to pay their last respects, listened and longed for Number 42, who had died too young, too soon.

The casket was placed in the hearse by pallbearers Ralph Branca, Larry Doby, Junior Gilliam, Don Newcombe, Pee Wee Reese, and basketball great Bill Russell. And then the funeral cortege slowly and solemnly moved its way through the streets of Harlem and Bedford Stuyvesant. Thousands lined the route. Sad-eyed, crying, some waved a final good-bye to the man who had enriched their lives. In Cypress Hills Cemetery, not far from where there was once a ball park named Ebbets Field, Jack Roosevelt Robinson was laid to rest.

Those who knew him best reach for the words to frame what he meant to them, what he meant to society:

"I put myself in Jackie's shoes," says Pee Wee Reese, who at first objected to playing on the same team with Robinson and who then became a loyal supporter. "I think of what it must have been like for him. I think of myself trying to make it in an all-black league. I know I couldn't have done it . . . but Jackie could take care of himself."

"In remembering him," says Rachel Robinson, "I tend to de-emphasize him as a ballplayer and emphasize him as an informal civil rights leader—that's the part that drops out, that people forget. My memories of him are very good, very satisfying to me."

Roy Campanella, his former Dodger teammate, recalls: "The more they rode him, the better Jackie played . . . the better he made us all play. He was something else."

"From time to time," his brother Mack observes, "I'm watching sporting events, and I look at the TV screen, and I see Jackie Robinson. I look at the whole spectrum of black America's life from 1947 on against 1900 to 1947. We're no longer the servants, the butlers, the maids. We're senators, congressmen, mayors. We are baseball managers. I trace it back to Jack's breaking the color line and creating a social revolution in a white man's world. Blacks have excelled in all areas because Jack and Branch Rickey showed the world we could."

EPILOGUE: IMPACT

7

On August 3, 1982, at the main post office in Brooklyn, New York, just a couple of blocks away from where Jackie Robinson and Branch Rickey had first met, a ceremony was staged. It was a ceremony to dedicate the Jackie Robinson Commemorative Stamp on its second day of issue.

I was there to make a speech. Others assembled for the occasion included Rachel Robinson, author Roger Kahn, former Brooklyn Dodger Gene Hermanski, Brooklyn Borough President Howard Golden.

When I reached the stage and stood behind the microphone, I decided to depart from the remarks I had prepared for the occasion. Others had praised Jackie Robinson; others had cited his record, his accomplishments. It seemed out of place for me to simply repeat what others had said. Therefore, I told a story that has been with me through all the long years and perhaps has been one of the reasons I have always been an admirer of Jackie Robinson.

For a while Jackie and Rachel lived in a house in Brooklyn in the East Flatbush section of the borough. One day my father and I drove out to the block, hoping to catch a glimpse of the man. I was just a kid, but my hero worship for Number 42 was very strong.

I don't know how long we lingered on the sidewalk across the street from the Robinson house. It may have been a half hour or so. Then I noticed the front door of the house open. Jackie came out. He must have noticed the shy kid and his father gaping from across the street. He raised his hand in greeting and motioned for us to come over. I don't remember what we said to each other. I remember shaking hands. I was too shy to ask for an autograph. The meeting was brief, but the memory of the friendliness and the warmth of that pressured man has been with me for a long time.

Over the years I have spoken to many people who knew Jackie Robinson well. They have confirmed that the same consideration he showed for a kid and his father was for him a way of life. In fact, it was Robinson who said, "A life is not important except in the impact it has on other lives."

If we take that as a way of measuring Jackie Robinson's life, despite the obstacles and hardships, the disappointments and tragedies, it was a life truly well spent—a life of impact.

Just as many whites became devoted followers of Reverend Martin Luther King, Jr., a whole generation of white people had their consciousness raised by Number 42. He was an underdog—especially at the start. He was only seeking equal rights and no special treatment—the opportunity to play major-league baseball and to be evaluated solely on his playing ability. He showed the world he could play the game: a .311 lifetime batting average, Rookie of the Year in 1947, and Most Valuable Player in 1949. In his nine-year career with the Dodgers, he averaged over one hundred runs scored each season. He was a first baseman, a second baseman, a third baseman, and an outfielder—versatility and verve were his trademarks.

As an athlete he had an astounding impact on the sport of baseball. There may have been greater performers in the long history of the game, but very few brought the dash and fire to it that he did or had to bear the burden he bore as a black pioneer.

His daring base-running, his clutch-hitting, his inside knowledge of the game and its rules, his will to win—these lifted him far above the average and into the category of the exceptional.

Many experts have remarked that if they had to select one player to start a team, that player would be Jackie Robinson, for all-around winning ability.

He came to play, to excel. Even though hurt, exhausted, discouraged, threatened, he played. He played when everything mattered, and he performed with the same intense desire when nothing mattered at all. In this way he was a model of sustained drive, of consistent excellence, of dedication to team, to profession, to prevailing.

His battling, brave image and his proficient, persistent ways created many Brooklyn Dodger fans and millions of Jackie Robinson rooters. How much he did to change people's stereotypes of blacks can never really be measured. Yet there are many today whose first realization of the plight of blacks and the nature of bigotry stems from their exposure to Jackie Robinson in a baseball uniform. And if they were fair-minded, their feelings went out to him.

The Jackie Robinson story is one of the bigger-than-life true happenings of the twentieth century. Armed with athletic skills and a determined character, he battled against loneliness and bigotry, against fame's glittering spotlight and its demands. He did not back down. He pressed on. This was another way his life had meaning—showing what determination and persistence can accomplish against great odds.

What he did was to change the way whites looked at blacks and the way blacks looked at themselves. And this was another, perhaps still not completely understood, part of his impact.

On the radio, in the newspapers, in the gossip on the streets, and later on television, what Jackie Robinson did on the ball field, what Jackie Robinson had to say, was covered in depth. For people of his race, he became a role model. He was one of their own, making good. He was one of their own, speaking out. One can only wonder what impact this had on the hopes and dreams of millions of black Americans. How many black Americans had their horizons widened because Number 42 showed that there was a possibility to succeed?

Not enough studies have been conducted to fully measure what he did and what his impact was on his race. However, how he changed the game of baseball is in the record books. In 1947 he was the only black man in the major leagues. By 1953 there were twenty-three spread over the rosters of seven teams. By 1959 the Boston Red Sox had signed Elijah "Pumpsie" Green, and every big league club had at least one black player. These men—the Monte Irvins, the Reggie Jacksons, the Lou Brocks, the Hank Aarons, the Willie Mays, the Bob Gibsons—borrowing a page from Number 42's book—brought a verve and a competitiveness to the national pastime that enriched the sport.

Today there are black coaches and black executives in baseball. There are black baseball managers—something Jackie Robinson was criticized for arguing for. Today all sports are enriched by the contributions of black athletes. And they do not have to go through the pain of breaking new ground. They simply take their places on the baseball fields, the football gridirons, the basketball courts—and if they can play the game, their way is assured. That is another one of the foundations built by Jackie Robinson.

There was still another manner in which Jackie Robinson had an impact on the world around him. As a product of the Southern legacy of slavery, the open world of California athletics, the untiring support of his mother, his sister, his brothers, and his wife, Jackie Robinson felt he had a responsibility to speak out against what he saw as injustice and unfairness.

"Life owes me nothing," he once said. "Baseball owes me nothing. But I cannot as an individual rejoice in the good things I have been permitted to work for and learn about while the humblest of my brothers is down in a deep hole hollering for help and not being heard."

Robinson was heard, and in being heard, he gave a powerful voice to those who until then had gone unheard. There were those who, during his major-league career and afterward, disliked him for his outspoken points of view. He cared not. Silence was not his way: popularity was not his goal.

Robinson responded to some native, inner drive. Some called him a "hothead." Others said he should keep his thoughts on race relations and politics to himself. His was the democratic way—a path he followed as a citizen and as a celebrity who felt deeply about his fellow human beings.

Today he remains the stuff of dreams, the striving for potential, the substance of accomplishment. Today he remains a powerful, driving symbol of a person with limitless athletic ability, the weight of his people on his soul, raging against a world he did not make, dying too young.

Today he remains for all those who saw him play . . . Number 42 in the uniform of the Brooklyn Dodgers . . . the pigeon-toed walk, the shuffled feet, the bluff, the dash, the stolen base, the crowd's roar . . . the impact lingering on through all the years.

APPENDIX:
THE RECORD

JACK ROOSEVELT ROBINSON

Led National League in stolen bases (39) 1947 and (37) 1949; hit for cycle (first game) August 29, 1948; led second basemen in double plays 1949 through 1952.

World Series Records—Tied record for assists by second baseman in one inning (3); seventh inning, October 8, 1949; tied for mark by getting four bases on balls in a game, October 5, 1952; one of 12 players to steal home in a World Series game, accomplishing feat in first game, eighth inning, September 28, 1955.

Named by The Sporting News as the Rookie of the Year in 1947.

Named as second baseman on The Sporting News All-Star Major League Teams, 1949-50-51-52.

Named Most Valuable Player, National League, 1949.

Named to Hall of Fame, 1962.

Year	Club	League	Pos.	G.	AB.	R.	H.	2B.	3B.	HR.	RBI.	B.A.	PO.	A.	E.	F.A.
1946	Montreal	Int.	2B	124	444	*113	155	25	8	3	66	*.349	261	385	10	*.985
1947	Brooklyn	Nat.	1B	151	590	125	175	31	5	12	48	.297	1323	92	16	.989
1948	Brooklyn	Nat.	INF	147	574	108	170	38	8	12	85	.296	514	342	15	*.983
1949	Brooklyn	Nat.	2B	156	593	122	203	38	12	16	124	*.342	395	421	16	.981
1950	Brooklyn	Nat.	2B	144	518	99	170	39	4	14	81	.328	359	390	11	*.986
1951	Brooklyn	Nat.	2B	153	548	106	185	33	7	19	88	.338	*390	*435	7	*.992
1952	Brooklyn	Nat.	2B	149	510	104	157	17	3	19	75	.308	353	400	20	.974
1953	Brooklyn	Nat.	INF-OF	136	484	109	159	34	7	12	95	.329	238	126	6	.984
1954	Brooklyn	Nat.	INF-OF	124	386	62	120	22	4	15	59	.311	166	109	7	.975
1955	Brooklyn	Nat.	INF-OF	105	317	51	81	6	2	8	36	.256	100	183	10	.966
1956	Brooklyn (a)	Nat.	INF-OF	117	357	61	98	15	2	10	43	.275	169	230	9	.978
MAJOR LEAGUE TOTALS				1382	4877	947	1518	273	54	137	734	.311	4007	2728	117	.983

Traded to New York Giants for pitcher Dick Littlefield and reported $35,000, December 13, 1956; Robinson announced retirement from game, January 5, 1957, canceling trade.

WORLD SERIES RECORD

Year	Club	League	Pos.	G.	AB.	R.	H.	2B	3B	HR.	RBI.	B.A.	PO.	A.	E.	F.A.
1947	Brooklyn	Nat.	1B	7	27	3	7	2	0	0	3	.259	49	6	0	1.000
1949	Brooklyn	Nat.	2B	5	16	2	3	1	0	0	2	.188	12	9	1	.955
1952	Brooklyn	Nat.	2B	7	23	4	4	0	0	1	2	.174	10	20	0	1.000
1953	Brooklyn	Nat.	OF	6	25	3	8	2	0	0	2	.320	8	0	0	1.000
1955	Brooklyn	Nat.	3B	6	22	5	4	1	0	0	1	.182	4	18	2	.917
1956	Brooklyn	Nat.	3B	7	24	5	6	1	0	1	2	.250	5	12	0	1.000
WORLD SERIES TOTALS				38	137	22	32	7	0	2	12	.234	88	65	3	.981

FOR FURTHER READING

Frommer, Harvey. *New York City Baseball: 1947-1957.* New York: Macmillan, 1980.

Recaptures the golden decade when the Giants, the Yankees, and the Dodgers were all home-based in New York City.

Begins with Jackie Robinson joining the Brooklyn Dodgers in 1947 and ends with the Dodgers and the Giants leaving the city for California at the end of the 1957 baseball season.

_____.*Rickey and Robinson.* New York: Macmillan, 1982.

A double biography of the men who together broke baseball's color barrier. The book focuses on the lives of both men, their disparate beginnings, and the cause that bonded them in their adult lives.

Kahn, Roger. *The Boys of Summer.* New York: Harper & Row, 1972.

An evocation of the Brooklyn Dodger years and the lives and fortunes of some of the players in their after-baseball careers. One chapter, "The Lion at Dusk," centers on Jackie Robinson.

Robinson, Jackie. *I Never Had It Made.* New York: Putnam, 1972.

Jackie Robinson's autobiography. His childhood in California, his army years, his baseball career, and the later period of his life when he was a spokesperson for the civil rights movement.

INDEX